C#

INTERVIEW QUESTIONS
YOU'LL MOST LIKELY BE ASKED

362
Interview Questions

VIBRANT
PUBLISHERS

C#

Interview Questions
You'll Most Likely Be Asked

ISBN-10: 1-946383-08-2
ISBN-13: 978-1-946383-08-2

Library of Congress Control Number: 2011901173

This publication is designed to provide accurate and authoritative information in regard to the subject matter covered. The author has made every effort in the preparation of this book to ensure the accuracy of the information. However, information in this book is sold without warranty either expressed or implied. The Author or the Publisher will not be liable for any damages caused or alleged to be caused either directly or indirectly by this book.

Vibrant Publishers books are available at special quantity discount for sales promotions, or for use in corporate training programs. For more information please write to **bulkorders@vibrantpublishers.com**

Please email feedback / corrections (technical, grammatical or spelling) to **spellerrors@vibrantpublishers.com**

To access the complete catalogue of Vibrant Publishers, visit **www.vibrantpublishers.com**

Table of Contents

This page is intentionally left blank.

C# Interview Questions

Review these typical interview questions and think about how you would answer them. Read the answers listed; you will find best possible answers along with strategies and suggestions.

This page is intentionally left blank.

Chapter 1

Introduction

1: How can you get input from command line?

Answer:

Console.Readline() is the command which prompts the user to enter the value for a variable or an argument. A sample example is as follows:

```
// Namespace Declaration
using System;
// Program start class
class UserInput
{
    // Main indicates the beginning of program execution.
    public static void Main()
    {
        // To Write in console OR To get input from Console
        Console.Write("Where are you from?: ");
```

```
        Console.Write("I am from, {0}! ", Console.ReadLine());
    }
}
```

On execution of above program prints "Where are you from?:" and waits for the user input. User should type the value and press enter key to continue.

2: Why do we need Command line input?
Answer:
Many windows utilities have some type of command line interface. When we type notepad filename.txt in command line, notepad will open the contents of your filename provided. Command line inputs facilitate to write scripts that can invoke the program to pass values through arguments.

3: How does shallow copy differ from deep copy?
Answer:
Deep copy:
   a) It is creation of new instance of an object
   b) It copies all fields and creates copies of memory allocation pointed to by the fields
Shallow copy:
   a) It is a bit wise copy of an object
   b) It holds the references to the same object and in other terms copies the address where the values are stored

4: What is a delegate in C#?
Answer:

Delegates are used to define methods callback. They are similar to the function pointer of C++. Methods can be passed as arguments using delegates.

Using delegates multiple methods can be invoked on a single event.

For example: int i = int.parse("99"); -

5: What is a sealed class?

Answer:

Class name prefixed with sealed keywords prevents the ability to inherit the properties and methods of the class. Methods of a sealed class can be called by creating objects for the class. Sealed keyword is similar to final keyword in Java.

Example for sealed class:

```
public sealed class mySealedclass
{
        public string name;
        public double quotation;
}
```

Creating object for a sealed class:

```
mySealedclass msc=new mySealedclass ();
```

6: How can you achieve multiple inheritance in C#?

Answer:

Multiple inheritance is not supported in C#. This can be achieved using Interface. Interfaces are classes where methods and properties can be defined.

Methods implementations will not be available within the class.

Also, an interface cannot be instantiated directly. Multiple interfaces are supported in C# as a replacement for multiple inheritance.

7: What is a reflection?

Answer:

Reflection is the ability to find information about objects. Compilers for languages such as JScript use reflection to construct symbol tables.

The namespace System.Reflection defines the Assembly, ParameterInfo, Enum, Module, MemberInfo, MethodInfo, Type, FieldInfo, ConstructorInfo, PropertyInfo, and EventInfo types to analyze the metadata of an assembly.

8: What is a metadata?

Answer:

Metadata contains a number of different tables; for example, a type definition table, a filed definition table, a method definition table, and so forth.

By parsing these tables, we can get an assembly's types and attributes.

9: Are nullable datatypes supported in C#? If No explain the reason for this, if Yes describe which property can be used to check of null value and which to get the value.

Answer:

C# supports nullable datatypes. Nullable types represent value type variables that can be assigned the value of null. A typical scenario for null datatypes is on databases that it contains elements that may be not assigned a value. You can assign a value to a nullable type the same way you assign a value to other value types, for example int? x = 10. HasValue and Value properties are used to test for null and retrieve the value respectively.

10: What are error types available in C#?
Answer:
Following are the error types in C#:
   a) Run-Time Error
   b) Parser Error
   c) Configuration Error
   d) Compilation Error

11: What is a Constructor?
Answer:
The following are the key points about a constructor:
   a) The method name is the same name as that of the class
   b) Never returns a value
   c) Can be overridden to provide custom initialization feature
   d) Get executed as first method when an object is created
   e) Used to initialize class and structure the data before use

12: What is the use of keyword static?
Answer:
A function/variable named with keyword static can be called using the class name and object creation is not required. Keyword 'this' cannot be used within a function which is defined as a static

function. Static constructors can be created in C#.

```
class MyClass
{
static MyClass()
{
// static construction code
}
```

In the above example, we have a static method MyClass() which gets executed whenever the class is loaded.

13: What is Dispose?

Answer:

Dispose method is used to release memory for an object. Dispose method is part of IDisposable interface.

Dispose method has no arguments and it returns void. If a class wants to declare publicly that it implements the Dispose() method, it must implement IDisposable

<Objectname>.dispose will release the memory.

14: What is enumeration?

Answer:

An Enumeration is a user-defined integer type. Enumerations make the code easier to maintain by ensuring that variables assigned are only legitimate. It also allows you to refer to integer values by descriptive names.

Example of Enumeration is mentioned below:

```
Public enum TimeOfDay
{
```

Morning = 0, Afternoon=1, Evening=2
}
Enumeration can be accessed as
TimeOfDay.Morning

15: What do you know about Enumeration Types? Why use an enumeration instead of a numeric type?
Answer:
An enumeration type can be used to define a set of named constants. One typical scenario is to define an enumeration type Days containing seven values each representing a day of a week. By default the underlying type of each element in the enum is int, however using a colon you can specify other numeric types such as byte. Enum keyword is used for the declaration of enumeration types. The advantages of using an enum instead of a numeric type is that you clearly set which values are valid for the variable and that it improves code readability.

16: Describe the differences between String and StringBuilder. When is it recommended to use a StringBuilder instead of a String object?
Answer:
String is an immutable type. Immutable means that an operation to String instance isn't executed on the same instance, but a new String is created instead. On the other side StringBuilder is a mutable type, meaning that all operations of modifying an instance such as remove, add, insert and other operations are executed on the same instance. StringBuilder should be used at

scenarios where performance is important, for example when an application needs to make significant number of changes to a string.

17: What is the use of keyword Monitor?

Answer:

Using Monitor, a particular section of application code can be blocked by other threads while the code is being executed. Object locks provide the ability to restrict access to a block of code, commonly called a critical section.

Monitor is associated with an object on demand. An instance of a monitor class cannot be created. It can be called directly from any context. Monitor class controls access to objects by granting a lock for an object to a single thread.

18: Compare values types with reference types.

Answer:

a) In value type, values are stored in stack and for reference type it is stored on heap.

b) When values types are not initialized default values will be 0, false. In case of reference type null will be set if not initialized.

c) Variables of value type contain values and reference types contain references.

19: What is an array and what are types are arrays available?

Answer:

Array is a collection of related instances. It can be reference or a value type. Arrays are zero indexed. Size of an array is fixed at instantiation. Array can be declared as type[] arrayName; The following are the types of arrays:

a) Single Dimensional
b) Multidimensional
c) Jagged

20: What is an unsafe code?

Answer:

Unsafe is a reserved keyword. Codes whose safety cannot be verified by the Common language Runtime is an unsafe code. CLR will execute only safe codes within the assembly. Typical example of unsafe code is usage of pointers.

Unsafe keyword can be used to define an unsafe context where pointers can be used. Unsafe code creates security and stability risks and also may increase applications performance. Unsafe code cannot be accessed inside an anonymous method.

21: What is the use of CopyTo?

Answer:

CopyTo is an array function. It creates a clone of the original array. This can be used only for single dimensional arrays. It copies a specific number of characters from the selected index to an entirely new instance of an array. Variable where CopyTo method is used should be of equal size or greater than the size of the original array.

```
void DisplayFile()
{
```

```
StringCollection lineCollection =
ReadFileIntoStringCollection();
string [] lineArray = new string[lineCollection.Count];
lineCollection.CopyTo(lineArray, 0);
this.textBoxContent.Lines = lineArray;
}
```

In the above example, the copyTo function is used for single dimensional array.

22: What is a namespace?

Answer:

Namespaces provide a way of organizing related classes and other types. Namespaces are logical grouping of classes. Namespaces can be nested as mentioned below:

```
Namespace CustomerInfo
{
    using system;

    public struct Subscriber
    {
    //code for struct here
    }
}
```

Namespace can be used by 'using' keyword.

Ex: using CustomerInfo;

23: Which is the base class of all classes in the .NET Framework? Please reference some methods of the class that can be

overridden. **What should you be aware of when using that class?**

Answer:

The base class used by all classes in the .NET framework is the Object class. The inheritance is implicit so you do not have to inherit from Object class. The methods that can be overridden are the following: Equals, Finalize, GetHashCode and ToString. Object class should be used when your requirement is to design a class that can handle any type of object. You should take into account the performance cost due to the process of boxing and unboxing.

24: What is a Partial class?

Answer:

A class which can span across multiple files can be achieved using Partial keyword.

Sample code snippet is as follows

```
//ClassFile1.cs
partial class ThePartialClass
{
      public void Method1(){
      }
}
//ClassFile2.cs
partial class ThePartialClass
{
      public void Method2(){
      }
}
```

When both the above two files are compiled in a single project, one single type ThePartialClass will be created with two methods.

25: What are static classes?

Answer:

A class with only static methods and properties can become a static class as mentioned below:

```
static class MyUtilities
{
    public static void MyMethod(){
    }
}
```

An object of type MyUtilities is not required to call the MyMethod(). The class name is used to make the call:

MyUtilities.MyMethod();

26: What are preprocessor directives?

Answer:

Preprocessor directives are meaningless when used alone. They become meaningful when used with other directives.

For example:

```
int DoSomeWork(double x)
{
// do something
#if SHOW
Console.WriteLine("x is " + x);
#endif
}
```

In the above code Console.WriteLine will get executed if SHOW is already defined using #define directive as #define SHOW. Otherwise it will not get executed.

27: List out the available preprocessor directives available in C#.

Answer:

Preprocessor directives constitute only command in a single line and are not terminated by; (semicolons).

The following are the list of preprocessor directives available in C#:

#define, #undef, #if, #elif, #else, and #endif, #region and #endregion, #line, #pragma

28: How do structs differ from class?

Answer:

Structs differs from classes through the way it is accessed and stored in the following ways:

a) Classes are of reference type. Structs are of value types
b) Classes are stored in heap. Structs are stored in stack.
c) Structs doesn't support inheritance
d) Structs are best choice for small data structures and gives better performance

29: Can we create alias for namespaces?

Answer:

Yes we can create alias names for namespaces. Alias names can be created by 'using' keyword and the typical example is as follows:

```
using AliasName = MynameSpace;
```

The reason why we go for alias is that it can be difficult where we use a nested namespace as explained below:

    using Appendix = BookCompany.Publisher.BookType;

In the above statement BookCompany is a main namespace and Publisher is a child namespaces of BookCompany and BookType is a child namespace of Publisher.

Chapter 2

Assemblies and Security

30: You are required to save the assemblies in a location where all the other computer applications can easily access them. Where should you add the assemblies?

Answer:

The assemblies must be added to the Global Access Cache. The assemblies located in the cache can be shared amongst various applications. The assemblies are located in the path 'Windows/WinNT' directory. Different applications can easily access the assemblies if placed inside the application directory. It is necessary to perform integrity check on assemblies when added to the cache.

31: There is a need to place the resource specific to a language in a different assembly. Which of the assemblies would help the user to add it?

Answer:

The satellite assemblies help in adding the resources for different languages to different assemblies. Once the application in specific language is selected, the related assembly is loaded from the memory. The satellite assemblies helps user to localize the assembly. All the satellite assemblies contain resources.

32: Discuss the different security mechanisms used in .NET?

Answer:

There are two security mechanisms used in .NET. They are:

a) Code access security

b) Validation and verification

In **Code Access security**, the evidence of the associated assembly is used. Using the access security, the permissions assigned to the code are determined.

Validation and verification mechanism is performed when the assembly is loaded in Common Language Runtime. In the validation process, the CLR checks for a valid metadata. The verification checks if the code is unsafe.

33: What are the different components of code access security?

Answer:

The components of code access security are:

a) .**Permissions:** The administrator is responsible for managing the user level and machine level permissions. The CLR Virtual System is used for loading and executing the program. The managed code is executed and the assembly metadata is used for connection.

b) **Code Group:** The code is added in a group for providing the permissions. The assembly which fulfills the condition is the member of the group.

c) **Evidence:** The different types of evidence provided to the CLR are Zone, Strong Name, URL, Publisher, Application Directory, Site, Hash Value.

34: What are assemblies?

Answer:

The DLL Hell issue in Microsoft platform is resolved by assemblies. The following are the key points about assemblies:

a) Assemblies can be EXE or DLL file with metadata information

b) It is a self-describing unit

c) It has one or more files

d) An assembly can be private or shared

e) Installation as easy as copying files that are related to assembly

35: What is a private assembly?

Answer:

Assembly being used by a single application is private. Private assembly will be stored in same folder of the application directory or a sub folder of it. Strong name is not required for identification of assembly.

User need not have to worry about registration, versioning if they choose private assembly. Other assemblies outside the application will not impact on the application.

36: What is a shared assembly?

Answer:

Assembly being used by multiple applications is called shared assembly. This should be stored in Global Assembly Cache. A technical example for a shared assembly is the .Net runtime classes.

Versioning constraints are enforced on shared assembly during run time. Strong name identification is required for shared assembly. Strong name has assembly's identity, version number, public key and digital signature.

37: What is a strong name?

Answer:

Strong name provides unique identification of assembly. Namespace collision problem can be solved using SN. Strong name enables side-by-side code execution. Strong names can be used during versioning and Authentication of the application. Authentication involves signature and public keys. Strong Name ensures disabling of creating subsequent version for the assembly. Assemblies generated using a private key will have a different name compared with the assembly generated with another private key.

38: What is a global assembly cache?

Answer:

GAC is the short form of Global Assembly Cache, which is a cache for globally available assemblies. Shared assemblies reside inside the GAC.

It is not mandatory that all assemblies should be placed in GAC and make is available for COM or unmanaged code. There are possibilities and scenarios where a private assembly can also be placed in the GAC.

39: What is a Native Image Generator?
Answer:

The Ngen.exe is nothing but the Native Image Generator. It helps you to compile the IL code to the native code during installation time. It installs the native image in NIC which is Native Image Cache. The primary location of Native image cache is <windows>\assembly\NativeImages<RuntimeVersion>.
Ngen helps to display all the assemblies from image cache with the display option. It gives all installed versions of this assembly and the dependent assemblies of the native assembly.

40: What is the use of a Global Assembly Cache Viewer?
Answer:

Using a windows shell extension shfusion.dll we could display the global assembly cache. Shfusion helps to manipulate and view the cache contents.
Global assembly cache viewer helps to view the Global Assembly name, culture, type, version and the public key token. Properties of an assembly can be viewed when an assembly is selected using context menu.

41: What is a Gacutil?
Answer:

In order to install and uninstall an assembly we have to go for gacutil.exe. There are several options available in gacutil to perform the actions in assembly.

To list all the assemblies from an assembly cache use

gacutil /l

To install shared assembly testdll into the assembly cache use

gacutil /i testdll

To uninstall an assembly testdll use

gacutil /u testdll

42: How can we create a strong name?
Answer:

A strong name is required for a shared assembly in order share across applications. Using SN (strong name) tool a strong name can be created. Using the following command, strong name can be created.

sn –k mysnkey.snk

For each project a key file can be created using sn tool. The key file will have the extension pfx. Upon rebuilding, public key file will be available in the manifest.

43: How can we install a shared assembly?
Answer:

In order to install a shared assembly in GAC we require a public key. The gacutil tool helps to install the assembly in GAC. The following command helps to create a shared assembly for the dll gacutil /i testdll

In order to install the assembly automatically after a successful build, one should configure a post-build event command line.

44: What is delayed signing of assemblies?

Answer:

If AssemblyDelaySign attribute is set to true, no signature will be stored in the assembly. An assembly cannot be tested without using a key and it cannot be installed in GAC. The following are the steps for delayed signing of assemblies:

   a) Using sn utility, create a public/private key pair
   b) Use the sn tool to extract the public key with –p option
   c) Verification of the signature should be turned off.
   d) Using sn tool assembly should be re-signed with –R option
   e) Installation as easy as copying files that are related to assembly

45: How can you extract a public key and re-sign an assembly?

Answer:

Use the following command to extract the public key

   sn –p mysnkey.snk mysnkeypk.snk

-p option extracts the public key and it will be stored in mysnkeypk.snk file.

The following command helps to re-sign on the delayed signed assemblies or a previously signed assembly.

   sn –R mynewassembly.dll mysnkey.snk

46: List out the types of settings available in configuration files.

Answer:

a) Using <startup> tag version of the runtime can be specified. Different version of runtime can be installed on the same system

b) Using runtime settings we can specify GC performed during run time. Version policy and code base can be specified using runtime settings

c) To configure applications using .NET Remoting, remoting settings can be used

d) Using security settings configuration of permissions and cryptography can be done

47: What are the various version parts of an assembly?

Answer:

An assembly has four parts for version number. Consider an assembly version 1.0.200.1100. The four parts are major.minor.build.revision.

If there are changes in build and revision versions, the assembly is considered to be a compatible version of previous version. Change in major or minor may be considered as incompatible with previous versions.

48: What is Code Access Security?

Answer:

CAS, short form of Code Access Security is one of the main features of .NET. CAS runs within a restricted environment. It manages code dependent on the permission levels given to the assembly. When there is an attempt to perform an action and if there are no relevant permissions available, a security exception will be thrown.

CAS ensures protection from malicious code. We can specify what part of code can access the database part and what part of code should not have access.

49: List out various types of code group membership conditions.
Answer:
   a) **Zone:** Is the region from which code is originated
   b) **Site:** Website from which code is originated
   c) **Strong: Name:** A verifiable, unique name for the code
   d) **URL:** A location from which code is originated
   e) **Hash Value:** Assembly hash value
   f) **Publisher:** Publisher of the code
   g) **Custom:** User defined condition
   h) **Application directory:** Location of the assembly

50: What is CASPOL?
Answer:
CASPOL is the short form of Command-line Code Access Security Policy tool. It helps to modify security policy at various levels like machine level, enterprise policy level and user policy level. CASPOL.exe helps to write batch scripts to configure security policy. A membership condition and permission set should be defined when we add a code group to a code group hierarchy.

51: List various commands available in caspol.exe.
Answer:

a) To get list of available options of the tool use
    - caspol.exe -?
b) To send output into a text file
    – caspol.exe > myfile.txt
c) To list the hierarchical structure of code group
    – caspol.exe –listdescription
d) Alternate for caspol.exe
    –listdescription is caspol.exe –ld
e) To view code access groups
    – caspol.exe –listgroups

52: List out the code access permission provided by CLR.
Answer:

a) DirectoryServicesPermission
b) DnsPermission
c) EnvironmentPermission
d) EventLogPermission
e) FileDialogPermission
f) FileIOPermission
g) IsolatedStorageFilePermission
h) IsolatedStoragePermission
i) MessageQueuePermission
j) OleDbPermission
k) PerformanceCounterPermission
l) PrintingPermission
m) ReflectionPermission
n) RegistryPermission
o) SecurityPermission

p) ServiceControllerPermission

q) SocketPermission

r) SQLClientPermission

s) UIPermission

t) WebPermission

53: What are the limitations of .NET security features?

Answer:

Unmanaged code is not being enforced on Security policy but still it provides protection against calls on unmanaged code.

When a user places an assembly in a local folder, security policy is bypassed as the assembly has FullTrust. This can be fixed by granting permission to local code.

Script based viruses and malicious code are least dealt by .NET security policy.

54: How can you create and manage code groups?

Answer:

Using caspol code groups can be created and permissions can be set.

a) To turn on and off the security

    caspol.exe –security off

    caspol.exe –security on

b) To reset security policy

    caspol.exe –reset

c) To remove a code group

    caspol.exe –remgroup 1.1.4

d) To change permissions

caspol.exe –chggroup 1.1.4 FullTrust

55: What do you know about Thread Pooling? Describe its usage and how it can be used in C# applications.

Answer:

A thread pool is a collection of threads that is used to execute several methods or tasks in the background. This results in enhanced user experience as the primary thread is free for performing other tasks. When a thread in the pool completes its task, it will return to a queue of waiting threads where it will be available for the next asynchronous task. The major advantage of thread pooling is that enables the reuse of threads, avoiding the cost of creating and initializing a new thread each time you want to perform an asynchronous task. In order to execute a method with thread pooling you have to call ThreadPool.QueueUserWorkItem method.

56: What is threading?

Answer:

Thread is an independent set of instructions in a program.
Threads in C#, is handled by class thread. Thread class is available in System.Threading namespace.
Parallel execution of code is supported through multithreading.
Multithreading is internally managed by thread scheduler which is a function of CLR which delegates to the operating system.

57: List out the threadstate values.

Answer:

a) **Running:** The thread has been started and not blocked

b) **StopRequested:** Thread being requested to stop

c) **Stopped:** The thread has stopped

d) **Suspended:** The thread has been suspended

e) **Aborted:** The thread is now dead and status not changed to stoped

f) **Background:** The thread is currently being executed in background thread

g) **Unstarted:** Thread.start not invoked on the thread

h) **AbortRequested:** Thread.Abort is invoked on the particular thread

58: What is the use of Threadpool?

Answer:

Threadpool class helps to reuse existing threads from a list of pool of threads Using Threadpool class is easier than using the Thread class.

Threadpool class can be used when the performance of how the application uses the threads is of high priority. Nearly 25 threads can be accesses using threadpool.

59: What is locking?

Answer:

Locking ensures that only one thread will be allowed to enter a particular section of a code at a time. Lock and Mutex are the two locking constructs available. Lock construct is more convenient and faster considered with Mutex. We can go for a SpinLock struck for a high-concurrency scenario.

Example usage of lock struck is as follows

```
class ThreadSafeLock
{
    static readonly object _mlocker = new object();
    static int _myval1, _myval2;
    static void Go()
    {
        lock (_mylocker)
        {
        if (_myval2 != 0) Console.WriteLine (_myval1 /
        _myval2);

        myval2 = 0;
        }
    }
}
```

Chapter 3

Data Access

60: User needs to access the data from the student table using the DataReader object. What code should beadded for accessing the rows from the table?

Answer:

The code for accessing the rows from the student table using DataReader object:

```
static void HasRows ( SqlConnection con )
{
    using ( con )
    {
        SqlCommand cmd = new SqlCommand ( "Select studid,
        studname from student;", con );
        con.Open();
        SqlDataReader dr = cmd.ExecuteReader();
        if ( dr.HasRows )
```

```
{
    while ( reader.Read())
    {
        Console.WriteLine("{0}\t{1}", dr.GetInt(32),
        dr.GetString(1));

    }
}
else
{
    Console.WriteLine("Rows not present");
    }
dr.Close();
}
}
```

61: What are the advantages of using the DataSet in a disconnected data structure?

Answer:

The different advantages of using the DataSet in a disconnected data structure are as mentioned below:

a) All the query results are saved in the DataSet using the SqlDataAdapter object. There is no connection between the database and DataSet

b) All the modifications done to the DataSet contents do not affect the database

c) Using the dataset class, user can easily pass the contents from a component to another in a multi tire application

d) The data in the dataset can be sorted and filtered and helps to view only the rows which satisfy the condition

62: There are two tables as orderdetails and productdetails in the database. User needs to access the results from both the tables. What C# code must be added to access the data?

Answer:

Using the NextResult method, user can access the data from multiple tables.

```
static void AccessMultipleData ( SqlConnection con )
{
    using ( con )
    {
        SqlCommand cmd = new SqCommand(
        "select orderid, quantity from orderdetails;" +
        "select productid, location from productdetails", con);
        con.Open();
        SqlDataReader dr = cmd.ExecuteReader();
        while ( dr.HasRows )
        {
            Console.WriteLine("\t{0}\t{1}", dr.GetName(0),
            dr.GetName(1));

        while ( dr.Read())
        {
            Console.WriteLine("\t{0}\t{1}", dr.GetInt16(0),
            dr.GetString(1) );

        }
        dr.NextResult();

        }
    }
}
```

63: What are the different data adapter events used for responding to the changes made to the data source?

Answer:

The data adapter events used for responding to the events are as mentioned below:

a) **RowUpdating:** The event is raised before the row is updated from the DataSet and is processed at the source. The event is used for changing the behavior before the update functionality is performed and also provides additional event handling. User can cancel the modification and reschedule the data. The RowUpdatingEventArgs arguments passed to the event contain Row property, command property, and a Statement Type property.

b) **RowUpdated:** The event is raised after DML operations are performed on the row. It is used for handling the exceptions and errors that occur in an update. The ContinueUpdateOnError property is used for handling the error for the updated rows.

64: List the namespaces used for data access.

Answer:

Following are the namespaces used for data access:

a) System.Data
b) System.Data.Common
c) System.Data.Odbc
d) System.Data.Oledb
e) System.Data.ProviderBase

f) System.Data.Oracle

g) System.Data.Sql

h) System.Data.SqlClient

i) System.Data.Sqltypes

65: List out the classes available in System.Data namespace.

Answer:

The following are the shared classes available under the
System.Data namespace:

a) DataSet

b) DataTable

c) DataRow

d) DataColumn

e) DataRelation

f) Constraint

66: List out the Data Specific classes available in C.

Answer:

a) SqlCommand, OracleCommand, OleDbCommand and
    ODBCCommand are used for executing Sql statements or
    Stored Procedures

b) SqlConnection, OracleConnection, OleDbConnection and
    ODBCConnection are used to connect to the database

c) SqlDataReader, OracleDataReader, OleDbDataReader and
    ODBCDataReader are used as forward only data reader

d) SqlCommanBuilder, OracleCommanBuilder,
    OleDbCommanBuilder, ODBCCommanBuilder are used
    to generate SQL statements

e) SqlParameter, OleDbParameter, OracleParameter,
    ODBCParameter are used to define parameter to stored
    procedures

67: Explain how to create and open a database connection.

Answer:

The following code explains how to create and open databsase connection.

```
using System.Data.SqlClient;

string db_source = "server=(local-server);" + "integrated
security=SSPI;" +
    "database=proj_maindb";
SqlConnection my_conn = new SqlConnection(db_source);
conn.Open();

// Do something useful
conn.Close();
```

68: What are the fundamental objects of ADO.NET?

Answer:

There are two fundamental objects available in ADO.NET. They are: DataReader and DataSet.

a) **DataReader** is a forward only recordset. Only read
    operation can be performed which helps to browse
    through the records and display it

b) **DataSet** is a two way recordset. Dataset is a collection of
    tables, fields and rows

69: What is the difference between DataReader and DataSet?

Answer:

a) DataReader is forward only and read only data access where as Dataset is can hold multiple tables

b) DataReader is a connected architecture whereas DataSet is disconnected

c) DataReader cannot persist contents whereas DataSet can

70: What is DataAdapter?

Answer:

DataAdapter acts as a bridge between DataSource and DataSet and is responsible for filling DataSet. DataAdapter can perform SQL Statements like Select, Insert, Update and Delete in the Data Source.

SqlDataAdapter, OleDbDataAdapter, OracleDataAdapter, ODBCDataAdapter are the various adapters available.

71: List the commonly used methods of DataAdapter.

Answer:

a) **Fill**: Executes Select statement to fill Dataset or DataTable. It can also used to refresh the DataSet
adapter.Fill(client, "Client");
The first argument is the object name and second argument is the table name.

b) **FillSchema:** It uses SelectCommand to extract schema of a table and creates an empty table

c) **Update:** Calls respective Insert, Delete, Update statements for the respective calls in the DataSet

d) **Equals:** Overloaded method which determines if the
   object instances are equal

72: Explain the various objects in DataSet.

Answer:

DataSet is a collection of DataTable, DataRow, DataColumn,
DataView objects. DataTable objects contain collection of
DataRow and collection of DataColumn objects. It also contains
primary keys, default values and constraints used in the table. It
also holds the relation between parent and child tables.

DataView is an object in which data can be searched and
manipulation of data also occurs while displaying the data.

73: What is a DataView?

Answer:

DataView represents a table or a portion of row depending upon a
condition. Using DataView data can be searched and sorted in the
DataTable. Following are the methods available in DataView
object:

a) **Find:** Accepts array of values and returns with index of
   the row
b) **Delete:** A specific row can be deleted from the DataView
c) **AddNew:** A new row can be added in the DataView
d) **Find Row:** It returns a collection of data row

74: List out the methods provided by Command Object.

Answer:

a) **ExecuteNonQuery:** Executes queries which does not

return any value. On completion of the execution it
returns integer value which represents the number of rows
affected

b) **ExecuteReader:** Method returns an object which is
    connected with the resulting row and allows the row to be
    retrieved

c) **ExecuteScalar:** Method returns a single row of data from
    the fetched dataset and discards the other rows and
    column values

75: Where should we write the connection strings?

Answer:

Connection strings should be stored as key value pair in
ConnectionString section of the Configuration element in
configuration file.

In Case of a web application it should be written in web.config
file. In case of windows application it should be written in
app.config file.

Typical app.config file is as follows:

```
<?xml version='1.0' encoding='utf-8'?>
    <configuration>
        <connectionStrings>
            <clear />
            <add name="StringName"
            provider="System.Data.ProviderName"
            dbconnectionString="Connection String;" />
        </connectionStrings>
    </configuration>
```

76: How can you retrieve a connection string by name?

Answer:

The following program is example to retrieve a connection string from a configuration file by providing the name.

```
// Retrieves connection string by the name.
// Returns null if name is not found.
static string ConnectionStringByName(string stringname)
{
    // Assume failure.
    string returnString = null;

    // Check for the name in the connectionString.
    ConnectionStringSettings mysettings =
        ConfigurationManager.ConnectionStrings[stringname];

    // If found, return the connection string.
    if (mysettings != null)
        returnString = mysettings.ConnectionString;

    return returnString;
}
```

77: Provide the connection strings for various Databases.

Answer:

SQL Server Connection string

```
    using System.Data.SqlClient;
    ...
    SqlConnection ObjSQLConn = new SqlConnection();
```

```
ObjSQLConn.ConnectionString = "Data Source=(local);" +
    "Initial Catalog=MySQLServerDB;" +
    "Integrated Security=SSPI";
ObjSQLConn.Open();
```

Oracle Connection String

```
using System.Data.OracleClient;

OracleConnection ObjOracleConn = new OracleConnection();
ObjOracleConn.ConnectionString = "Data Source=Oracle9i;" +
    "Integrated Security=SSPI";
ObjOracleConn.Open();
```

ODBC Connection string

```
string myODBCConnString = "DRIVER={SQL
Server};SERVER=MyDBServer;Trusted_connection=yes;DATA
BASE=myDB;";
```

78: What is ExecuteXmlReader?

Answer:

ExecuteXmlReader is another method of command object. It executes a command and returns an XmlReader object and traverse through the XML elements.

Following is a sample program where ExecuteXMLReader is used:

```
using System;
using System.Data.SqlClient;
using System.Xml;


public class ExecuteXmlReaderSample
```

```
{
    public static void Main(string[] args)
    {
        string Dbsource = "server=(localserver);" +
            "integrated security=SSPI;" +
            "database=MyDBName";
    string Sqlselect = "SELECT Name,Company " +
    "FROM Customer FOR XML AUTO";
        SqlConnection DBconn = new SqlConnection(source);
        DBconn.Open();
        SqlCommand Sqlcmd = new SqlCommand(Sqlselect,
        DBconn);
    XmlReader Objxr = Sqlcmd.ExecuteXmlReader();
    Objxr.Read();
    string str;

    do
    {
                str = Objxr.ReadOuterXml();
                if (str!="")
                Console.WriteLine(str);
        }
        while (str!= "");
        conn.Close();
        }
}
```

79: Give a sample program for ExecuteReader method.

Answer:

```
public class ExecuteReaderSample
{
    public static void Main(string[] args)
    {
string DBsource = "server=(localserver);" +
"integrated security=SSPI;" +
"database=MyDbName";
        string Sqlselect = "SELECT Name,Company FROM Customer";
        SqlConnection objconn = new SqlConnection(Sqlsource);
        objconn.Open();
        SqlCommand objcmd = new SqlCommand(Sqlselect, objconn);
SqlDataReader objreader = objcmd.ExecuteReader();
while(objreader.Read())
{
Console.WriteLine("info : {0,-10} Company : {1}",
objreader[0] , objreader[1]);
}
    }
}
```

80: What are the various options available in ExecuteXmlReader Method?

Answer:

ExecuteXmlReader object has FOR XML AUTO, FOR XML RAW, FOR XML EXPLICIT options.

  a) **FOR XML AUTO:** It builds a tree structure based on tables mentioned in FROM clause

  b) **FOR XML RAW**: From the result sets, maps the rows to

elements and columns to attributes

c) **FOR XML EXPLICIT:** The shape of the xml tree should be specified for this option to return

81: How can you call a Stored Procedure?

Answer:

Stored Procedures can be called using Command object by defining the store procedure and adding definition for the parameters and executing the command method.

SqlCommand objCommand = new
SqlCommand("ExampleUpdate", conn);

objCommand.CommandType = CommandType.StoredProcedure;
objCommand.Parameters.Add(new SqlParameter ("@ID",
SqlDbType.Int, 0, "ID"));
objCommand.UpdatedRowSource = UpdateRowSource.None;
objCommand.ExecuteNonQuery();

82: Define DataColumn.

Answer:

DataColumn defines properties of a column. DataColumns can be used to create data types Boolean, Decimal, Int64, Byte, Char, Double, Single, String, DateTime, Int32. Datacolumn object has several properties and they are:

a) AllowDBNull

b) AutoIncrement

c) AutoIncrementSeed

d) Caption

e) ColumnMapping

f) ColumnName

g) DataType

h) DefaultValue

i) Expression

83: Define DataRow.

Answer:

The actual data of a data table can be accessed using DataRow object.

Following sample code fills the dataset and iterates using DataRow

```
SqlDataAdapter objda = new SqlDataAdapter(sqlselect,
objconn);

DataSet objds = new DataSet();

objda.Fill(objds , "Customer");

foreach(DataRow objrow in objds.Tables["Customer"].Rows)

Console.WriteLine('"{0}'
```

84: How can you populate a Dataset?

Answer:

Dataset can be populated in two ways:

a) **Using a data adapter**

```
SqlDataAdapter objda = new SqlDataAdapter(sqlselect
, objconn);

DataSet objds = new DataSet();

objda.Fill(objds , "Customer");
```

b) **Read XML into the dataset**

```
DataSet objds = new DataSet();
objds.ReadXml(".\\Data.xml");
```

85: How can you insert a new row in a DataTable?

Answer:

New row can be inserted into a DataTable in two ways:

a) A NewRow() method can be called to add a new row

```
DataRow objrow = objds.Tables["readlog"].NewRow();
objrow["ID"]=129;
objrow["Description"]="Test Record";
objds.Tables["readlog"].Rows.Add(objrow);
```

b) Rows.Add() method can be used to add a new row. We have to pass an array of values to the rows.

```
DataRow objrow = objds.Tables["readlog"].Rows.Add
(new object [] { 123 , "Test Record" });
```

86: How can you update a row in the DataTable?

Answer:

a) Using the datarow object, either index name or index number can be specified and assigned with a replacement value

```
objrow["Description"]="replace text";
objrow[1] = "new value";
```

b) To update the database from DataAdapter use update() method

```
objda.Update(objds , "readlog");
```

87: What are the methods available in the dataset to generate XML?

Answer:

a) **ReadXML:** Reads a XML document into Dataset

b) **GetXML:** Function which returns the string containing XML document

c) **Writexml:** Writes a XML data to disk

88: Can we load multiple tables in DataSet?

Answer:

Yes, multiple tables can be loaded in DataSet. Below is the sample where multiple tables are loaded using DataAdapter object.

```
objCmd.CommandText = "FirstTable"
objDa.Fill(objDS, "FirstTable")
objCmd.CommandText = "SecondTable"
objDa.Fill(objDS, "SecondTable")
```

The below code returns value from a particular table

```
listdata.DataSource = objDS.Tables("FirstTable").DefaultView
```

This page is intentionally left blank.

Chapter 4

Keywords

89: What different C# modifiers are used in programming?

Answer:

The C# modifiers used in programming are as mentioned below:

a) **The access modifiers:** public, private, protected and internal are used for declaring the accessibility of the types and members

b) **async:** Used for defining the lambda expressions, anonymous methods and modified methods

c) **event:** The events in C# can be declared

d) **const:** The constants defining the value of the variable which cannot be changed

e) **new:** The member inherited from the base class is hidden

f) **partial:** A partial class is defined. The structs and methods in the same assembly are defined

g) **sealed:** The class which cannot be inherited is defined

h) **override:** The implementation of the virtual member which is derived from the base class

i) **static:** The member which belongs to the type and not the particular object

90: What is the use of namespace and what different types are added to it?

Answer:

The namespace is useful for adding a set of related objects related to the scope. The elements are used for arranging the code elements and unique data types are created. The different types added to the namespace are as mentioned below:

a) **class:** The class is used for inheriting the implementation from the base class. More than one interface can be implemented in a class. The members of class can be protected, public, private, protected internal, or internal.

b) **interface:** The methods, properties, events or indexers can be added in the interface declarations. The members declared in the interface definition must be implemented in the class or struct.

c) **delegate:** The delegate type is same as the methods signature. It is a reference type and is useful in encapsulating the anonymous methods.

d) **enum:** The enumeration is declared using enum. The set of named constants are added in the enumerator list.

e) **struct:** A struct type is used for encapsulating similar variables. The fields, methods, indexers, operators, events, constructors, constants are added in the structure.

91: What is the use of null keyword in C#? Explain through an example the use of null keyword.

Answer:

A null is a simple text known as literal which is used for referencing a null reference. It is always used as a reference type in C# programming. User can assign the null keyword to class, method, objects, array, and value type.

The following example demonstrates the use of null keyword:

```
class Demo
{
    public static void Main(string[] args)
    {
        Demo dc ;

        //Assign the variable as null
        dc = null;

        dc = new Demo();

        //Compare two string using the null keyword

        string s1 = null;
        string s2 = String.Empty;

        bool b1;
        b1 = s2.Equals(s1);
        Console.WriteLine(b1);
```

```
        Console.WriteLine("The string is", s1 == s2? "Is equal":
        "Not Equal");

        Console.ReadLine();

    }

}
```

92: Sam needs to explicitly convert the double data type to int data type. What code should be added to achieve the conversion?

Answer:

Using the explicit keyword, user can covert the data type. The following code snippet demonstrates the type conversion.

```
class Demo
{
    static void Main()
    {
        double d = 1234.5;
        int i;

        i = ( int) d;
        Console.WriteLine("The value of integer is", i );
    }
    Console.Read();
}
```

93: Which keywords can you use in order to specify how a method in a derived class interacts with a method with the same name in a base class?

Answer:

When you want to extend a base class the keyword override should be applied on the derived class. At common inheritance scenarios this is the desired behavior, you want instances from the derived class to be able to use the methods in the derived class and not the ones defined in the base class. On the other side when you require to hide a member inherited from the base class the new keyword should be used.

94: What is the difference between Shadowing and Overriding?

Answer:

Shadowing: Hides member of a base class member in the derived class using the 'New' keyword.

```
class DerivedClass: BaseClass
{
double var1,var2;
public new doubleDerivedfun()
{
//Sample code;
}
}
```

Overriding: Overriding is the concept of same function name with same signatures and same return type. Virtual keyword should be used in base class and override keyword should be used for derived class function for overriding.

```
class DerivedClass: BaseClass
{
double var1,var2;
public overrride doubleDerivedfun()
{
//Sample code;
}
}
```

95: Describe the is and as operators and their usage
Answer:

a) **IS operator:** is used to check if the run-time type of an object is compatible with a given type. An is operator applied on an expression would be true only if the expression is not null and can be casted to the provided type successfully.

b) **AS operator:** is used when you need to convert compatible types, for example at inheritance types. When this conversion is not feasible, as operator will not throw an exception but will return null instead.

96: List the access modifiers available in C#.
Answer:

Access modifiers are keywords that are used to specify the accessibility of a member. The following are the available access modifiers:

a) Public

b) Protected

c) Internal

d) Private

e) Protected Internal

97: Explain Protected Internal access modifier.

Answer:

Any class should contain only one access modifier except the Protected Internal modifier.

Access of members is limited with the current assembly or to the derived class members in the same assembly. Access modifiers are not allowed for namespaces.

98: What is an internal access modifier?

Answer:

Classes named with access modified internal can be accessed only within the files in an assembly. If an attempt is made to access the member of base class in an external file, it will throw an error.

File1.cs

```
internal class mybaseclass
{
// Do something useful
}
```

File2.cs

```
class myaccess
{
public static void main()
```

```
{
    Mybaesclass myobj = new mybaseclass();
}
}
```

The above program throws an error as we are trying to access the internal class from a different class in a separate file.

99: What is a private access modifier?

Answer:

Private access modifier is the least permissive level. Members of type private are accessible within the class body. Members of a class are private by default.

```
using System;
class user
{
    public string username = "name";
    double salary = 5000.00; // private access by default
    public double GetSalary() {
        return salary;
    }
}
```

In the above sample code, private member salary can be accessed using public function only.

100: What is a protected access modifier?

Answer:

Protected member can be accessed within the class and from within the derived classes. The protected member of a base class can be accessed by class type of the derived class. If an attempt was made by a class type of base class to access the protected member in derived class will throw an error.

```
class BaseClass
{
    protected int xyz = 100;
}


class ChildClass : BaseClass
{
    void Fun()
    {
        BaseClass objbase = new BaseClass();
        ChildClass objchild = new ChildClass();
        objbase.xyz = 10; // Error
        objchild.xyz = 10; // Correct
    }
}
```

101: What is a public access modifier?

Answer:

A class and member can be set to public access type. This is the most permissive level. There is no restriction for any public members on access. Any class can access the public member of another class using the object.

```
using System;
class Base
{
```

```
        public int xyz;
        public int abc;
    }

    class Class2
    {
        public static void Main()
        {
            Base objB = new Base();

            objB.xyz = 10;
            objB.abc = 15;
            Console.WriteLine("xyz = {0}, abc = {1}", objB.xyz,
            objB.abc);

        }
    }
```

102: What is boxing?

Answer:

Boxing is the process of converting a value type into object or to an interface type.

When the Common Language Runtime boxes a value type, the value is wrapped inside system.object and stores it on heap.

```
    int i = 123;
    // Boxing i.
    object obj = i;
```

103: What is unboxing?

Answer:

The process of extracting the value type from an object is called unboxing. Boxing is an implicit call whereas unboxing is explicit. During unboxing the object instance is a boxed value of the given type.

    obj = 123;
    i = (int)obj; // unboxing

104: Explain about the keyword Virtual.

Answer:

The keyword Virtual is used to modify a method declaration or a property. Members or methods followed by keyword Virtual are called Virtual method or virtual member. When a method is declared as virtual, it can be overridden by the derived class. Virtual modifier cannot be used with static, abstract and override keywords for members or functions.

    public virtual double Calculate();

105: Explain about Volatile keyword.

Answer:

Volatile keyword indicates a field can be modified by operating system, a thread or by the hardware.

Volatile is set to fields which are accessed by multiple threads. It ensures one thread retrieves the latest value updated by another thread.

    class myClass
    {
        public volatile int xyz;
        Test(int _xyz)

```
    {
        xyz = _xyz;
    }
    public static void Main()
    {

    }
}
```

106: What are the restrictions for volatile keyword?

Answer:

The keyword volatile has restrictions with the following types:

a) Any reference types

b) Types like sbyte, byte, uint, bool, float, char, short, ushort

c) Enum type with an enum base type as bool, byte, sbyte, int, uint, short, u short

d) Pointer types

107:.Explain about readonly keyword.

Answer:

Readonly is a modifier which can be used on fields. Fields with modifier keyword can have assignments as a part of the declarations or by a constructor in the same class.

```
    public readonly int xyz = 10;


    public class ReadOnly
    {
        class ClassName
        {
```

```
        public readonly int xyz = 100;
        public readonly int abc;

        public ClassName()
        {
            abc = 24; // readonly
        }
    }
}
```

108: Describe the keywords used in C# for exception handling.

Answer:

C# provides an easy to use mechanism for handling any exception that may occur during the execution of your code. Exception handling mechanism is implemented by the following keywords:

a) **throw:** used to notify that an exception has occurred,

b) **try-catch:** consists of a try block followed by a clause. You can also have more than one clauses. Each catch clause defines the way to handle each type of exception. The try block contains the code that may cause the exception and that we want to protect from throwing an unhandled error,

c) **try-catch-finally**: same logic as try-catch with an addition of finally keyword. The statements inside a finally block will run when program control leaves a try statement or after an exception is handled inside the catch block.

109: List out the constraints of override modifier.

Answer:

Overriding property declaration should specify the same access type and the name as the inherited property. The overridden property must be set to abstract, virtual or override.

An override method cannot have the new, virtual, abstract and static modifiers.

110: What is the use of the keyword const?

Answer:

Const keyword specifies that the value of the variable or the field cannot be modified. It introduces one or more constants for a given type.

    public const double a = 10.0, b = 25.5, c = 3.0;

Static modifier cannot be used in a const declaration.

111: What is the difference between readonly and const keywords?

Answer:

a) Const can be initialized at the declaration of the variable. Readonly can be initialized during the declaration or using a constructor.

b) Depending on the constructor Readonly variable can have different values. Const variables are compile time constants and readonly variables are runtime constants.

c) Static keyword can be used for Readonly type where static keyword cannot be used in const variables.

112: Explain about the event keyword.

Answer:

Event keyword allows you to specify a delegate that will be called during the occurrence of an event in the code.

```
using System;
public delegate void TestDelegate(); // delegate declaration

public interface myInterface
{
    event TestDelegate MyEvent;
    void myfuc();
}
```

113: Explain the steps that need to be followed in order to create and use events.

Answer:

The steps that need to be followed in order to create and use events are:

a) Create a delegate. There should be a delegate to use with event keyword when we define our own event. If it is a predefine event, then name of the delegate should be available to end users

b) Create a class that has an event created from the delegate. There should be a method to call the event. The method can be overrides of some base class functionality

c) There should be one or more classes that will connect methods to the event. These classes will include associate of one or many methods using -= or += operators

d) Use the event to create an object of class that contains the event declaration

114: Explain about implicit keyword.

Answer:

Implicit keyword can be used to declare implicit user defined conversion operator.

```
class MyImplicitType
{
    static public implicit operator int(NewImplicitType m)
    {
        // code for converting from NewImplicitType to int
    }
}
```

Conversion operators are called implicitly without explicit casts.

```
NewImplicitType xyz;

int i = xyz; // implicitly call NewImplicitType's
NewmplicitType-to-int conversion operator
```

115: Explain about explicit keyword.

Answer:

Explicit operator can be used to declare an explicit user defined conversion operator.

```
class NewExplicitType
{
    public static explicit operator NewExplicitType(int xyz)
    {
```

```
        // code for converting from int to NewType
    }
}
```

Explicit should be used if a conversion operation causes exception.

Explicit operators must be invoked by a cast.

```
int xyz;

NewExplicitType x = (NewExplicitType)xyz; // int-to-
NewExplicitType requires cast
```

116: What is side-by-side execution?

Answer:

A .NET application compiled using one version of a .NET framework can run on a different version of .NET framework. The application can run on a system which has multiple versions of .NET framework installed. The application work based on the version using which the application was compiled.

A constraint in this side-by-side execution is that ADO.NET between different releases can affect forward and backward compatibility.

117: What is forward compatibility?

Answer:

The ability of an application to run successfully on a latest version of the .NET framework is called as forward compatibility. The application compiled in an older version may work without any issue in the latest version of .NET framework.

ADO.NET code of .NET framework version 1.1 can work with

latest versions of .NET framework which is forward compatible.

118: What is backward compatibility?

Answer:

Backward compatibility is the feature of an application in which the application was compiled in the latest version of .NET framework and it successfully runs on the older versions of the .NET framework.

The newly added features of the .NET framework may not be compatible with older versions of the .NET framework and the new feature is not a backward compatible feature.

119: What is interoperability?

Answer:

Interoperability helps to preserve and take advantage of the existing investments in the unmanaged code. Code which is being managed and controlled by the CLR is the managed code. Code that runs outside the CLR is called unmanaged code.

COM, COM+, Activex Components and Win32 API are examples of unmanaged code.

Using System.Runtime.InteropServices namespace, .NET Framework enables the interoperability with the unmanaged code.

120: What is Friend Assemblies?

Answer:

Assembly which has the ability to access another assembly's friend(VB) or internal(C#) type and members is an friend assembly.

Only assemblies which as explicitly specified as friends can access another assembly type and members.

InternalsVisibleTo attribute can be used to identify the friend assemblies for a given assembly.

This page is intentionally left blank.

Chapter 5

Windows Applications

121: What is use of event handling in windows forms. How can it be defined?

Answer:

Event handlers are used for handling events that occur when a program is executed. Event handling is used with Windows forms for handling the functionality and responding to the user. The delegates are used for declaring the events. The reference to the methods are present in the events.

The declaration and use of delegate is as coded below:

```
public delegate void DemoEventHandler ( int );
public event DemoDelegate DemoEvent;
```

Next, the event handlers are added to the event. They are matched with the delegate type of the event and the others are executed when the event is performed. The signature of the event handler must be similar to the event.

```
public void DisplayData ( int no )
{
    MessageBox.Show ("Welcome User!!!");
}
```

Attach the event using the += operator.

```
DemoEvent += new DemoEventHandler ( DisplayData );
```

The event is activated by calling the following method.

```
DemoEvent ( 10 );
```

122: A windows form contains three textboxes for Name, Age and location. Define the code for the event handlers used for transferring the data in the read only boxes.

Answer:

```
private void btn1_Click ( object sender, EventArgs e )
{
    string display;

    display = "Name" + this.txt1.Text+ "\r\n";
    display += "Age" + this.txt2.Text+ "\r\n";
    display += "location" + this.txt3.Text+ "\r\n";
}


private void btn2_Click ( object sender, EventArgs e )
{
```

```
        string display;
        display = "Your Name is \r\n";
        display += "Your Age is \r\n";
        display += "Your location is \r\n";
}
```

123: There is a textbox on the form which displays the value entered by the user. We need to validate the textbox using an event handler. Add the code for achieving the functionality.

Answer:

```
private void txtValidate_Validating ( object sender,
System.ComponentModel.CancelEventArgs e)
    {
        TextBox txt1 = ( TextBox ) sender;

        //If there is no value in the textbox, user validates it with
        the background color

        if ( txt1.Text.Length == 0 )
        {
            txt1.BackColor = color.Blue;
            txt1.Tag = false;
        }
        else
        {
            txt1.BackColor =
            System.Drawing.SystemColors.Window;
            txt1.Tag = true;
        }
```

```
//User can call the ValidateAll() method for assigning the
value


ValidateAll();
}
```

124: List the various dialog control used in the Windows forms application.

Answer:

The different dialog boxes used in the form application are:

a) **The ColorDialog Control**

Various colors can be selected from the ColorDialog control. It is available in the System.Windows.Forms.ColorDialog namespace. The properties like Color, AllowFullOpen, CustomColors, and FullOpen can be used for assigning them on the controls.

b) **The FolderBrowserDialog Control**

The FolderBrowserDialog control is used for browsing the directory available in the system. A tree structure is used for displaying the data. User can create new folders in the Browse For Folder window.

The properties like RootFolder, Description, SelectedPath and ShowNewFolderButton are useful for adding the details, path, defining the root folder.

c) **The FontDialog Control**

Different fonts can be selected using the FontDialog control. The dialog control is available in the System.Windows.Forms.FontDialog namespace. User can easily change the color, size, font and effects on the text to be displayed.

d) **The SaveFileDialog Control**

The control is used to save and write the content to the file. User can navigate through the files available in the system, and add the name of the file in which the data is added. User can add the complete path of a file in the FileName textbox.

The properties of the SaveFileDialog control are FileName, Filter, FilterIndex, AddExtension, CheckFileExists. These properties are useful are used for adding additional functionalities like name of the file, checking if the file is valid, filtering the files.

e) **The OpenFileDialog Control**

The OpenFileDialog control helps users to open and read text data from the file. Users can select the file from the system or add the whole path of the file.

The properties of the OpenFileDialog control are AddExtension, DefaultExt, FileName, Multiselect, Title, etc. They are used for adding extension, name of the file, selecting multiple options, adding title to the dialog.

125: How to create a Windows Form Application?

Answer:

The following code creates a blank window form:

```
public class MyWinForm : System.Windows.Forms.Form
{
    public MyWinForm()
```

```
    {
    }
    [STAThread]
    static void Main()
    {
        Application.Run(new MyWinForm());
    }
}
```

The statement Application.Run creates a blank window form.

126: What are the user interaction keywords associated with events?

Answer:

a) User interaction events are Click, Double Click, KeyPress, KeyDown, Paint and Validating. Mouse events are Click, DoubleClick, MouseUp, MouseDown, MouseHover, MouseLeave and MouseEnter.

b) The order of the key events is KeyDown, KeyPress and KeyUp.

c) Some of the field events are Enter, GetFocus, LostFocus, Validating and Validate.

127: How can we create non rectangular window?

Answer:

To create non rectangular window, first we have to create a rectangular form.

The Form has TransparentKey property which needs to set to the

BackColor of the form which will make the background as transparent.

Form has FormBorderStyle property and set it to FormBorderStyle.None which removes the contour and contents of form.

128: What are the form methods which control its lifecycle?

Answer:

The following form methods control its lifecycle:

a) **Constructor:** Form object is created using the constructor

b) **Layout:** Form is loaded and the layout is initialized

c) **Paint:** Form gets activated and paint is called

The reverse process of it is:

a) Form closes the application

b) Form gets deactivated

c) Dispose is called for de-allocation

129: List out the user defined Data types.

Answer:

Data types created by the user are user defined data type. They are distinct type with common representation or a structured type with sequence of named attributes. They following are the categories of User Defined Data Types:

a) Distinct Type

b) Structured Type

c) Reference Type

130: Explain about the various configuration files.

Answer:

Different types of configuration files available are:

a) **Machine.config**: This contains details of installation settings

b) **App.config or Web.config:** Helps to modify the default settings of machine.config file

c) **Security.config**: Helps to set machine level security settings

d) **Enterprisesec.config:** Sets enterprise level security policies

131: List the debugging windows available.

Answer:

Following are the windows that are available while debugging:

a) BreakPoints

b) Output

c) Watch

d) Autos

e) Local

f) Call Stacks

g) Modules

h) Threads

i) Immediate

j) Memory

k) Processes

l) Registers

m) Disassembly

132: What is the event of AddHandler Keyword?

Answer:

Using AddHandler event we can specify an event handler which can be used to handle events from a structure or shared events. AddHandler accepts arguments like the name of the event from event sender and an expression which evaluates to a delegate.

133: How can we throw a custom exception?

Answer:

We can throw a custom exception in the following ways:

a) Use try-catch-finally format needs to be followed for custom exception handling

b) Define a customException and inherit the Exception or from ApplicationException class

c) Define three constructors for the customException class each with different arguments

```
class customException : ApplicationException
{
    public customException() : base() {}
    public customException(string str) : base(st) {}
    public customeException(string str, Exception ae) : base(st, ae) {}
}
```

The above code throws a custom exception called Application Exception.

134: What are the deployment features of .NET?

Answer:

Following are the deployment features of .NET:

a) Isolation of applications and the elimination of DLL conflicts

b) Controlled sharing of code

c) Components of applications that are deployed are private by default

d) Enterprise deployment facilitates ease of distribution

e) Option to choose side-by-side versioning when multiple versions are available

f) On the fly update option to update the DLLs of remote computers

g) Advertising, repairing, publishing and install-on-demand are other features

h) Partially trusted code used by code based identification

135: How can we create an array?

Answer:

Array treats several items as single collection. Array can be created in the following ways:

a) Declaring reference to an array

     Int32[] arr;

b) Create array of 50 Int32elements

     arrB = new Int32[50];

c) Creating 2-dimensional array

     Double[,] arrC = new Double[20, 40];

d) Creating 3-dimensional array

     String[,,] arrD = new String[10, 20, 30];

136: What is WCF?

Answer:

WCF is the short form of Windows Communication Foundation. It is an SDK to develop and deploy services on windows. It provides runtime environment for services and helps to expose CLR types as services.

WCF is part of .NET 3.0 and it requires at least .NET 2.0 to run the application.

It extends the capabilities of Microsoft Distributed System technologies, Remoting, Enterprise services, Messaging, ASMX and other features.

137: What are the components of WCF?

Answer:

WCF is composed of three components:

a) **Service Class**: It implements the required service

b) **Host Environment**: Provides environment to host the service

c) **Endpoints**: These are connection points to connect to the service. Clients find endpoints through components like service contract, binding and address

138: What is the difference between array and arraylist?

Answer:

Following are the differences between array and arraylist:

a) Arrays are fixed length where are ArrayList are of variable length

b) Arrays are compiled strong type collection whereas

Arraylist are flexible and it can accommodate any data type

c) Array performance is faster compared to Arraylist as boxing and unboxing done in it affects the performance

139: Can we create custom controls?

Answer:

Custom controls can be created by enhancing features of current control. In order to change ReadOnly property of a Textbox control, derive from the control and override the property.

```
public new bool ReadOnly
{
    set {
        if(newvalue)
            this.BackgroundColor = Color.Green;
        else
            this.BackgroundColor =
            Color.NewColor(NewColor.Window);
        base.ReadOnly = newvalue;
    }
    get { return base.ReadOnly;}


}
```

140: List out the attributes that can be added for custom controls.

Answer:

The following attributes can be added for custom controls:

a) BrowsableAttribute

b) BindableAttribute

c) CategoryAttribute

d) DefaultValueAttribute

e) DefaultEventAttribute

f) DefaultPropertyAttribute

g) DescriptionAttribute

h) DesignOnlyAttribute

141: What is Bit Array?

Answer:

Bit array can merge array of bit values and values are Boolean in nature. Some of the properties of Bit Array are as follows:

a) **Item:** Gets or Sets values at specific position

b) **Count:** Gets number of elements available in BitArray

c) **Length:** Gets of Sets number of elements

d) **IsReadOnly:** Get a value which indicates whether BitArray is read-only

142: How do we access crystal reports?

Answer:

When crystal reports are integrated data can be accessed by ADO Driver, ODBC Drivers, excel and XML. Getting data from ODBC drivers are called as pull technology.

In pull method, data source can be selected using the wizard and the required fields from table can be selected to display in report. In push method data is selected during run time and it is passed to the report.

143: Explain the steps required to implement crystal reports.

Answer:

Following steps are required to implement crystal reports:

a) Click on Project Menu, select Add New Item >> Reporting >> Crystal Reports

b) Click Add button and on the window appears select choice based on the requirement. Once it is selected, choose the DB connection as OLE DB and use the wizard to choose the db and select the table

c) From the selected table choose the fields required to display and click finish

d) Click Create New Project and place a Crystal report viewer and define the report source

e) When the report source is selected, click OK and when you run the project, report will be displayed

144: Explain the difference between CTS and CLS.

Answer:

Each language in .NET has its own data type and they have various declaration styles. CTS define how we declare variables and use during run time. In C++ we have long data type and in VB we have integer data type. CTS converts these data types to System32 which in turn is a data type of CTS.

CLS is a subset of CTS. Any language which needs to use Common Language Interface should communicate with other CLS-complaint languages. This is based on set of rules laid by CLS.

145: What is the use of SCM?

Answer:

SCM is the short form of Service Control Manager. Following are the responsibilities of SCM:

a) It accepts requests to perform install and uninstall of windows services

b) Helps to start windows services

c) Enumerate installed windows services

d) Maintaining status information of the currently running service

e) To transmit control messages

f) To lock/unlock the windows service database

146: What is a MaskedTextBox?

Answer:

It provides validation mechanism for the user input in a form. If the text box needs to accept a specific format, then we can set masking in MaskedTextBox. Some of the properties are as follows:

```
MaskedTextBox MyMaskedTextBox = new MaskedTextBox();
MyMaskedTextBox.Text = "My MaskedTextBox";
MyMaskedTextBox.Name = "Dynamic MaskedTextBox";
MyMaskedTextBox.Font = new Font("Verdana", 16);
MyMaskedTextBox.Mask = "00/00/0000";
```

147: What are the components of Crystal Reports?

Answer:

Following are the components of Crystal Reports:

a) **Report Files**: The .rpt or report file should be distributed which can be either compiled (embedded) or independent from the application

b) **Crystal Reports merge module**: This ensures that correct report components and component versions are installed with the application

c) **.NET Framework**: It is required that the client machine should have the .NET framework

148: How to cast string to any data type?

Answer:

Assume MyInt as string data type and MyStr as integer.

```
Mystr="65"
MyInt=CInt(Mystr) --> Valid
MyIntn=Integer.parse(Mystr)--> Valid
```

In the above code, we used Integer.parse method to cast string to any data type.

149: List the fundamental objects of ADO.NET.

Answer:

Following are the fundamental objects of ADO.NET:

a) Connection, IDbConnection

b) Command, IDbCommand

c) DataReader, IDataReader, IDataRecord

d) DataAdapter, IDataAdapter

e) Parameter, IDataParameter, IDbDataParameter

f) Transaction, IDbTransaction

150: List the elements of .NET Framework.

Answer:

Following are the elements of .NET framework:

a) **CLR:** Common Language Runtime

b) **.NET Framework Class Library**

c) **CLS:** Common Language Specification

d) **CTS:** Common Type System

e) **WebForms**

f) **Data and XML**

g) **XML Webservices**

151: Explain about shrinking session state.

Answer:

To store data we have two options and they are:

a) Out of process session state

b) MSSQL Server Session state

```
<sessionState mode="SqlServer" sqlConnectionString="data
source=dbserver;Initial Catalog=aspnetstate"
allowCustomSqlDatabase="true" compressionEnabled="true" />
```

152: What is Garbage Collection?

Answer:

The process in which the CLR claims memory which are no longer required and not referenced by any object is Garbage Collection. When the objects loses its final reference values stored in heap will be garbage collected.

The garbage collection time is determined by the CLR. Memory of stack is cleared when the stack frame where their declaration ends.

153: What is the role of Garbage Collector? Which method forces an immediate garbage collection of all generations?

Answer:

The role of garbage collector it to manage the allocation and release of memory for your application. That provides an automated way and makes development possible without having to worry about when to free memory. Whenever you create a new object, a memory from the heap is allocated by CLR. As long as address space is available in the managed heap, the runtime will continue to allocate space for new objects. When the garbage collector needs to release memory it will check for objects in the heap that are no longer used by the application. GC.Collect method forces an immediate garbage collection of all generations.

154: How to display a number as percent?

Answer:

A number with any type may be displayed as a percent when we display it in the output. The following lines of code explain this

```
decimal vardec = 155.554;
string str = vardec.ToString("P2");
```

The output is

155.55%

155: How can we force to collect GC?

Answer:

It is possible to force Garbage collection using GC.Collect().
It is also required to run finalizers of the object which needs to be deallocated. We have to use GC.WaitForPendingFinalizers() in

addition to the GC.Collect in order to avoid finalizers method to be executed separately.

156: Explain how garbage collection manages reclamation of unused memory.

Answer:

CLR performs the GC functionality on small and large objects separately. Separate heaps are maintained for these two objects. CLR uses the JIT compiler which provides the references of objects indicating that objects are live. The other objects will be available for GC.

The free memory is merged and occupied memory is compacted and so the live objects are contiguous.

157: What is break mode?

Answer:

Break mode allows us to locate the error by observing the code line by line. A snapshot of the application which is running will be taken and values and status of each variables is stored in break mode.

There are several options to step through the code and they are:

  a) Step Into
  b) Step Over
  c) Step Out
  d) Run to Cursor
  e) Set Next Statement

158: What is WPF?

Answer:

   a) WPF is the short form of Windows Presentation
       Foundation.

   b) It allows us to create applications with rich look and feel.
       It supports design engine which allows users to make
       creative interfaces and applications with 3D images,
       animation which are not available in HTML4.

   c) It is a resolution independent and vector based rendering
       engine.

   d) WPF extends the core features which includes XAML

159: List the different documents supported in WPF.

Answer:

The documents supported by WPF are fixed and flow documents.

   a) Fixed documents can be used for WYSIWYG applications

   b) Flow document basically concentrate on optimize viewing
       and readability than giving simple fixed layout. It adjusts
       the contents based on values during runtime variables
       which include size and resolution

160: What is XAML?

Answer:

XAML is short form of Extensible Application Markup Language.
It is a declarative markup language which simplifies creating a UI.
XAML files are xml file which has .xaml extension.

The following code denotes how to create button as part of UI.

```
<StackPanel>
    <Button Content="Login"/>
```

</StackPanel>

161: What is Windows Workflow Foundation?

Answer:

a) It is a common framework for developing workflows into Window application which might coordinate interactions among people, among software or both.

b) Workflow foundation is part of .NET 3.0 frameworks.

c) It helps applications to define, execute and manage the workflows and it includes workflow engine, design tools and namespace which can be used with windows client and server versions.

162: What is LINQ?

Answer:

a) LINQ is the short form of Language Integrate Query.

b) LINQ is part of .NET framework 3.5. It supports querying capabilities in the .NET languages.

c) It integrates the database model into the programming model.

d) SQL statements of C# can be used to retrieve data and logic can be used for the same.

163: What are different areas in which LINQ can be used?

Answer:

LINQ can be used in the following:

a) **Linq to objects:** It represents querying collections which implement IEnumerable interface

b) **Linq to ADO.NET:** Linq to SQL, linq to DataSet, linq to Entities

c) **Linq to XML**

164: Explain about Register Directive attributes.

Answer:

There are three register directive attributes:

a) **TagPreFix:** This identifies the group to which the user control belongs to

b) **Namespace:** Contains controls that are about to be registered with custom control assembly

c) **Assembly:** It consists of custom controls

165: Will the *finally* block get executed, if an exception occurs?

Answer:

Finally block will get executed irrespective of the exception has occurred or not. *Finally* helps to ensure that some cleanup is done. This can be used to free resources which are used in try block.

```
        try
    {
        //some code here
    }
    catch (System.IO.IOException e)
    {
        Console.WriteLine("Message {0}. Message = {1}", path,
        e.Message);
    }
    finally
```

```
{
        //clear resource here
}
```

In the above code, finally code gets executed irrespective of an exception occurs or not.

166: How can we throw an exception?

Answer:

Exception can be raised by throw keyword.

```
using System;
class MyCustomException
{
    static void Main()
    {
        int xyz = 0;
        int myTemp = 0;
        try
        {
            myTemp = 104/xyz;
            Console.WriteLine("Some message here");
        }
        catch(DivideByZeroException dbze)
        {
            Console.WriteLine("Error message here");
        }
        finally
        {
```

```
        Console.WriteLine("The Result is {0}", myTemp);
    }
  }
}
```

167: What is JSON.Net?

Answer:

JSON.NET is an open source JSON framework for .NET. Features of JSON.NET are as follows:

a) Converts JSON to and from XML

b) This is faster compared to .NET's built in JSON serializers

c) Supports .NET frameworks 2.0, 3.5, 4.0, Window phone, Silverlight and windows 8 metro

d) Flexible JSON serializer converting between .NET objects and JSON

168: How do you split a string based on a character without using string.split function?

Answer:

System.Text.RegularExpressions namespace should be imported to use Regex.Split() method.

```
class Program
{
    static void Main()
    {
        // String with numbers.
        string strsentence = "10 fruits, 20 chocs, 40 icecreams.";
        // Get all digit as strings.
```

```
string[] myDigits = Regex.Split(strsentence, @"\D+");
foreach (string myValue in myDigits)
{
    // Parse the value.
    int num;
    if (int.TryParse(myValue, out num))
    {
        Console.Write (myValue);
    }
}
}
}
```

169: What is ELMAH?

Answer:

a) ELMAH is the short form of Error Logging Modules and Handlers which provides application wide error logging capability.

b) It can be added to .NET web application dynamically without need for re-compilation or deployment.

c) Unhandled exceptions can be logged to file system, database, and event log or email the details.

170: Explain briefly how Passport authentication works.

Answer:

Following steps explain how passport authentication works:

a) Install Passport SDK

b) Set applications authentication mode to Passport in the

web.config file

c) Set the authorization to deny the unauthorized users

d) Use PassportAuthentication_OnAuthenticate event to access user's passport profile and authorize the user

e) To remove passport cookies implement a sign-out procedure

171: What are the different ways in which WCF can be hosted?

Answer:

WCF can be hosted in the following ways:

a) **IIS Hosting:** Most commonly used technique and supports only http protocol

b) **Self Hosting:** Hosting either in console/windows application or also in windows service

c) **WAS Hosting:** Windows Activation Service Hosting

d) **Windows Service Hosting:** Service can be set to start when windows starts

172: What is ABC in WCF?

Answer:

a) **Address:** A stands for Address and it indicates where your service is present. Depending on the location and service http, tcp etc., it is hosted the address varies

b) **Binding:** B stands for Binding and it specifies how it should be communicated by the client

c) **Contract:** C stands for Contracts. Operation provided by the service is exposed here

173: List the various contracts of WCF.

Answer:

Following are the various contracts of WCF:

a) **Service Contracts:** WCF service should have at least one service contract

b) **Data Contracts:** Defines data exchanged between client and service

c) **Fault Contracts:** Used to handle errors in service

d) **Message Contracts:** Defines way messages are transferred through SOAP messages

174: How can we achieve method overloading in WCF?

Answer:

OperationContract property can be used to achieve this.

```
[ServiceContract]
interface ICal
{
    [OperationContract(Name="Add2num")]
    int Add(int abc,int xyz)

    [OperationContract(Name="AddDouble")]
    int Add(double abc,double xyz)
}
```

175: What are Destructors?

Answer:

a) Destructors are used to destroy object once they are used. They are represented by a tilde ~. Destructors cannot have return type and they take no parameters.

b) Any class can have only one destructor.

c) Destructors cannot be called and they are invoked automatically

d) It cannot be defined in structs.

e) It implicitly calls the Finalize on objects base class.

```
class myClass
{
    ~myClass() //destructor
    {
    }
}
```

Chapter 6

Web Application

176: Peter needs to create a web application for displaying the Welcome message to the user. What steps does he need to follow to achieve this task?

Answer:

The steps performed for the creation of web application for viewing the message are:

a) Open the Visual studio application in your system.

b) Select a new project and from the installed templates option, select Visual C# option

c) From the C# templates, select the MVC web application template

d) Add an appropriate name to the project, also add corresponding location where the file is saved

e) In the controller.cs class, add the following code.
   public class Controller1: Controller

```
{
    public ActionResult Index()
    {
        ViewBag.Message = "Welcome User";
        return View();
    }
}
```

f) Execute the code by pressing F5 or click Start Debugging option.

177: Explain in detail about the MVC architecture in C# web application.

Answer:

Using the Model View Controller (MVC) user can differentiate the model and user interface. The Model View and Controller are the three objects of the architecture.

a) **Model:** The processing related to the database is performed using the model component. The representation of the data is not handled by model. The data is passed to the view and the views can modify the look. The management of code is much easy with the model component.

b) **View:** The representation of data is handled by view. The data operations are not performed. There can be more than one view and they are controlled by the controller. The view can contain WML, HTML, XML, XSLT, web forms, etc.

c) **Controller:** The controller is used for handling the request from the input devices and pass the data to model and view. The user inputs trigger the event for changing the model for updating the state and notify the view to change its display.

178: What different controllers are present in the MVC hierarchy of an application?

Answer:

In the MVC controllers hierarchy, the folder consists of classes used for maintaining the input and resources. User can add appropriate names to the new added controllers. The Controller word must be added at the end of the name. The role of controllers is to process the input request, revert back to the client when the request is processed and save the processed data. The MVC framework is used for mapping the URL to the respective methods.

The HomeController is the default controller present in the controller folder. The Index and About are the two controls added to it.

179: Joe needs to pass the parameter from the controller to the view in the MVC architecture. What code should be added to transfer the values in the architecture?

Answer:

The steps for passing the values from controller to view are as mentioned below:

a) Open the Visual Studio application in your system and select the MVC web application template from the C#

templates.

b) In the HomeController.cs class, add the following code:

```
public ActionResult About()
{
return View();
}
```

c) In the solution explorer window, from the Controllers, right click and select Add Controller option. Add an appropriate name to the controller.

d) In the new added controller, add the below mentioned code.

```
public ActionResult Pass1( string data, int no = 5 )
{
    ViewBag.Text = data;
    ViewBag.No = no;
    return View();
}
```

e) Right click in the above function and add a new view to the application. Inside the view add the following code for displaying the values present in the ViewBag.

```
@{
    ViewBag.Title = "Pass1";
}

<h2>Pass1</h2>
<ul>
    @for ( int x = 0; x < ViewBag.No; x++)
    {
```

```
        <li>
                @ViewBag.Text;
        </li>
    }
    </ul>
```

f) Execute the program the loop will be executed and the output will be displayed.

180: What is the difference between ASP and ASP.NET?

Answer:

ASP:

a) ASP is interpreted while ASP.NET is compiled

b) ASP uses VBScript. So the ASP pages are interpreted

ASP.NET:

a) ASP.NET can use .NET languages C# and VB which are compiled to the Microsoft Intermediate Language (MSIL)

b) Web server controls available in ASP.NET helps to develop interactive applications

181: What is IIS?

Answer:

IIS is the short for of Internet Information Services created by Microsoft to develop internet based applications. IIS is a webserver where web applications can be developed and deployed which handles the requests and response on the applications deployed.

IIS supports email server like SMTP and also Frontpage server extension to get dynamic features of IIS.

182: Explain about ASP.NET file.

Answer:

ASP.NET pages are developed as .aspx file. An ASP.NET file can contain:

a) Processing instructions to the server
b) Code in C#, VB.NET, Jscript.NET and all .NET supported languages
c) Client side scripts
d) ASP.NET server controls.
e) Contents and Forms as HTML

183: What is an ASP.NET web form?

Answer:

ASP.NET controls on a page provides plenty of flexibility, and features similar to Windows Forms classes. The HTML contents of a web page is called Web Forms in ASP.NET

To combine all the code in one file <script> elements helps with two attributes.

```
<script language="c#" runat="server">
// Server-side code.
</script>
```

runat="server" instructs ASP.NET engine to execute the complete code in server instead of the client.

184: List out the ASP.NET page life cycle stages.

Answer:

Any .NET page goes different stages during before and after a request and the stages are as follows:

a) Page Request
b) Start
c) Initialization
d) Load
e) Postback event handling
f) Rendering
g) Unload

185: List out the various ASP.NET page life cycle events.

Answer:

During each stage of the cycle of a page, events are raised which can be used to handle our own code. For a control event, we can bind an event handler to the event. Pages in turn have several events and they are listed below:

a) PreInit
b) Init
c) PreLoad
d) Load
e) InitComplete
f) LoadComplete
g) Control Events
h) PreRender
i) Render
j) PreRenderComplete
k) Unload
l) SaveStateComplete

186: Explain about the PreInit event.

Answer:

PreInit is raised after the stage Start is finished and before the initialization stage starts. PreInit can be used for the following scenarios:

  a) Creating dynamic controls
  b) Setting a dynamic master page
  c) Setting the Theme Property dynamically
  d) Use IsPostBack property to check whether it is the first time the page is being processed. Set IsCallBack and IsCrossPagePostBack properties the same time.
  e) Set profile property values

187: Explain about Page Request Stage.

Answer:

This stage occurs before the start of the page life cycle. When a page is requested, ASP.NET decides whether the page needs to be compiled and parsed or a cached version of the requested page can be sent as response without running the page.

And for this reason it starts at the beginning of the page.

188: What is a PostBack?

Answer:

When a page is being loaded it determines if it is a postback or not. An example for a postback is when a click event of a button in the page causes a reload of the page, the page being loaded for first time is not a post back.

IsPostBack is a page property which indicates if the page is being loaded for first time and returns a Boolean value.

```
Protected void Page_Load(object objsender, EventArgs obje)
{
    //check for postback
    if (Page.IsPostBack)
        MyLabel1.Text = "Yes post back.";
    else
        MyLabel1.Text = "NOT a post back.";
}
```

189: What is caching?

Answer:

Caching is the process or technique to store the frequently visited pages in memory so that for consequent access it can be rendered from the cache instead of loading the page. The response for a page will be served from the content stored in the memory.

A cached web page contents freezes only if the cache from the server is cleared. If cache is not cleared after adding a new content, the page would keep showing the old content.

190: List out the different types of caching available in ASP.NET.

Answer:

a) **Output Caching:** It caches the output from the response. Timing of the cache lifetime can be specified in seconds for better performance.

```
<%@ OutputCache Duration="90"
VaryByParam="mystate" %>
```

b) **Fragment Caching:** It caches only a porting of the page generated by the response. We can specify the portion of a page using

```
<%@ OutputCache Duration="180"
VaryByParam="SectionID;FeatureID"%>
```

c) **Data Caching:** Caching of objects programmatically.

```
Cache['City']= dscities;
```

191: Explain about the stage Initialization.

Answer:

During the page initialization stage, controls on a page are available and a UniqueID property is allocated for each control in the page. Themes and a master page may also be applied to the page if applicable.

If the page is a post back, the post back values has not been loaded and also the values for the control property have not been restored from the view state.

192: What is a ViewState?

Answer:

VIewState allows storing the state of the objects in a hidden field on a page. ViewState is transported from the server to the client and this is not stored in the server or in any other external source. It helps to maintain the state of the server side objects between the postbacks.

```
if (ViewState["myserviceCookie"] == null)
{
//do something here
}
```

ViewState are similar to storing information at session level or application level.

193: What is HttpHandler?

Answer:

HttpHandler is a low level response and request API to service the incoming Http Requests. The IHttpHandler interface is implemented by all the handlers. The interface uses the System.web namespace and no other specific namespace is required.

A class that implements the IHttpHandler processes the incoming Http request received by ASP.NET. IHttpHandlerFactory handles the resolution of url requests raised to the IHttpHandler instances. Developers can create and register factories to support the rich request resolution in addition to the default IHttpHandlerFactory.

194: How can we improve the performance of ASP.NET page?

Answer:

The performance of ASP.NET page can be improved in the following ways:

    a) Turn off sessionstate, if it is not required
    b) Turn off tracing
    c) Disable viewstate of a page
    d) Set debug=false in the web.config
    e) Avoid Response.Redirect
    f) Try using string builder to concatenate strings
    g) Avoid throwing exceptions

h) To kill resources, use finally method

i) Use client side scripts for validation

j) User Page.IsPostBack

k) Use caching

l) Use Paging

m) Reduce the number of web server controls

n) Avoid using unmanaged code

o) Design with value types

195: What is the use of GLOBAL.ASAX file?

Answer:

Global.asax file resides in the root directory of the application. It is accessible by the application and cannot be accessed in the web and it is used by the application. It has collection of handlers that can be used to change and set the settings in the site.

Events can come from the HttpApplication object and any of the HTTPModule object which is specified in web.config or machine.config.

196: What are user controls and custom controls?

Answer:

A control which is authored by a user or by a third party software provider and does not belong to .NET framework library is a custom control.

A custom server control and client control is used in web forms and windows forms applications respectively.

A server control that is user authored enables an ASP.NET page and can be re-utilized as server control. User control persists as a file with .ascx extension and it is authored declaratively.

197: What is a session and application object?

Answer:

Using session object user specific information can be stored in the server.

    Session["MyUserData"] = "Store data";

Application object can be used to store the application specific information in the server

    Application["MyAppData"] = "Global value";

198: List the different types of directives available in .NET.

Answer:

Following are the different types of directives available in .NET:

 a) @Page

 b) @Control

 c) @Import

 d) @Implements

 e) @Register

 f) @Assembly

 g) @OutputCache

 h) @Reference

199: How can you prevent a browser from caching an ASPX page?

Answer:

SetNoStore method of HttpCachePolicy object can be called on the

Response Objects Cache property. Below is the sample code to prevent browser from caching the page content.

```
<%@ Page Language="C#" %>
    <html>
        <body>
            <%
                Response.Cache.SetNoStore ();
                Response.Write ("Prevented browser
                caching");
            %>
        </body>
    </html>
```

200: List out the validation controls available in ASP.NET.

Answer:

There are six validation controls available and they are:

a) **RequiredFieldValidator:** User cannot skip the entry

b) **CompareValidator**: Compares value against a constant value

c) **RangeValidator**: Checks user entry with the lower and upper boundaries range set by the field

d) **RegularExpressionValidator**: Checks whether the entered value matches an regular expression

e) **CustomValidator:** Checks with the custom validation specified.

f) **ValidationSummary**: Shows summary of all error Messages

201: What are the types of cookies available in ASP.NET?

Answer:

ASP.NET supports two types of cookies.

a) **Single valued**

> Request.cookies("mycookievariable")="myvalue";

b) **Multi valued**

> Request.cookies("userinfo")("name")="My Name";

202: List out the authentication techniques available in ASP.NET.

Answer:

There are three ways to authenticate a user and they are:

a) **Windows Authentication:** Users should have Windows Account

b) **Form Authentication:** Website has users registered from which it handles the request

c) **Passport Authentication:** Microsoft's centralized authentication service

203: What is smart navigation?

Answer:

Smart Navigation can be explained with the following points:

a) It retains the last page navigation in browser history

b) It eliminates flash caused during the navigation

c) It persist the scroll position during the postbacks between pages

d) It persist the element focus during postbacks

204: What is State Management in ASP.NET?

Answer:

The process by which a state of a page and page information is maintained for multiple requests of same or different pages is State Management. The two types of State Management are as follows:

a) **Client Side State Management:** This method stores the user information in user client machine in the form of cookie, url or embedding information into a webpage

b) **Server Side State Management:** The information is stored in server machine

205: List the different ASP.NET controls.

Answer:

ASP.NET has several controls which are grouped under the following control groups:

a) Standard Controls

b) Validation Controls

c) Data Controls

d) Navigation controls

e) Rich Controls

f) Login Controls

g) HTML Controls

206: List the techniques available to store the state information in Client Side State Management.

Answer:

a) **View State**: This is used to track the values in the controls. Custom values can be added to the view state. It automatically saves the value of the page

b) **Control State:** Control state is used to block other users from being changing the view state of the custom control

c) **Hidden Fields:** Stores values of HTML fields without showing it in the browser

d) **Cookies:** Stores values in user's machine. It can be used where the stored values needs to be used across multiple pages

e) **Query Strings**: Passing values in the URL which are visible to the user

207: What are the features of Grid View control?

Answer:

Following are the features of Grid View control:

a) Grid View provides facility to add sorting, paginated editing functionality with no coding required

b) PageSetting property supports Numeric, Next Previous, NumericFirstLast, Next PreviousLast

c) GridView supports Rowupdating and RowUpdated events

d) GridView supports Post-operations and Pre=Operations

e) It has AutoFormat support

208: List out the features of Data Grid.

Answer:

Following are the features of Data Grid:

a) Each row of record in Data Grid is displayed as a row in a table

b) It has built in support for Filter, Sort and pagination of data

c) It has predefined editing controls

d) AlternatingItemStyle, EditItemStyle, FooterStyle, HeaderStyle, ItemStyle, PagerStyle, SelectedItemStyle are the control styles available in Data Grid

e) HeaderTemplate, EditItemTemplate, ItemTemplate, FooterTemplate are the control templates available in Data Grid

209: What is a master page?
Answer:

a) Master page acts as a base and contents of all the pages are presented. Using master pages, multiple pages of consistent look can be created.

b) Pages which provide the contents that are displayed in a master page are the content pages.

c) Master page has a place holder where the contents of each page will be displayed.

210: What is the difference between callbacks and postbacks?
Answer:

a) Callback is the way to send a request to web page from client script. Postback involves expensive call with a processing overhead.

b) In callback, a request is sent by a client function and a method is invoked on the server.

c) Postback is the event that sends form data to the server. The returned value from the server is rendered on the browser.

d) ICallbackEventHandler, RaiseCallBackEvent and GetCallBackResult needs to be implemented to have client side callbacks.

211: How to copy contents of one dropdown list control to another dropdown control?

Answer:

Using the following code values of one dropdown can be copied to another dropdown control

```
foreach (ListItem item in mydropdown1.Items)
{
        mydropdown2.Items.Add(item);
}
```

212: What is the use of AspCompat attribute?

Answer:

AspCompat is an attribute of @Page directive. The default value of AspCompat is false. It should be set to true where COM object registered as ThreadingModel = Apartment.

```
<%@ Page AspCompat="true" %>
```

It facilitates ASP objects to be available to the COM components through placing unmanaged wrappers. It improves the performance of the calls.

If the page does not use any COM object it is recommended not to set AspCompat to true.

213: How to load a control dynamically during runtime?

Answer:

The following code is useful to add a control to a page form

```
Control objcon =
(Control)Page.LoadControl("~/usercontrols/UserControl.ascx");

Page.Form.Controls.Add(objcon);
```

Instead of adding to a page form, control could be added to a Panel which helps to place the control in the required position. The following code helps to place the control in a panel.

```
MyPanel1.Controls.Add(objcon);
```

214: Is it possible to get authentication mode during runtime?

Answer:

```
System.Web.Configuration.AuthenticationSection Objsection =
(AuthenticationSection)WebConfigurationManager.GetSectio
n("system.web/authentication");

MyLabel1.Text = Objsection.Mode.ToString();
```

The above code helps to get the authentication mode from the web.config file

215: List the event handlers that can be included in Global.asax file.

Answer:

Following event handlers can be included in Global.asax file:

   a) Application_Start,Application_End,

b) Application_BeginRequest,

c) Application_Disposed,

d) Application_AcquireRequestState,

e) Application_AuthorizeRequest,

f) Application_AuthenticateRequest,

g) Application_Error,

h) Application_EndRequest,

i) Application_PreRequestHandlerExecute,

j) Application_ResolveRequestCache,

k) Application_UpdateRequestCache,

l) Application_PreSendRequestContent,

m) Application_ReleaseRequestState,

n) Session_Start,Session_End

o) Application_PostRequestHandlerExecute,

p) Application_PreSendRequestHeaders

216: What is the difference between ResolveUrl and ResolveClientUrl?

Answer:

a) **ResolveUrl:** Returns a relative URL to the site root by using the control's TemplateSourceDirectory property

b) **ResolveClientUrl:** It Returns the URL relative to the folder which has the source file from which control is instantiated

It is good to use ResolveUrl which returns the relative url that can be across anywhere in a website.

217: Explain the AdRotator control.

Answer:

AdRotator is a control used to display ad images and on clicking will navigate to another web location. Ad images are loaded from a formatted XML document.

The XML document contains details about the ads such as the image to be placed, navigation links with which the details are displayed.

218: List the elements of the AdRotator file.

Answer:

a) **ImageUrl**: The advertisement image url which can be absolute or relative

b) **AlternateText**: This is an optional parameter which displays text on hovering mouse over the image

c) **NavigateUrl**: The destination url where the page needs to be taken to. If there is no navigateUrl set, then the image will not be clickable

d) **Impressions**: Another optional parameter which holds the weight of the order of images to be displayed

e) **Keyword**: It is an optional parameter which has the keywords

219: Is it possible to pass multiple querystring parameters with hyperlink?

Answer:

The following code explains how to pass multiple querystring parameters with hyperlink

```
<asp:HyperLink ID = "myhlClientId" runat = "server"
NavigateUrl = '<%# "TestPage.aspx?myparam1 = "
& _DataBinder.Eval(Container.DataItem, "myparam1")
& _"&myparam2 = " & DataBinder.Eval(Container.DataItem,
"myparam2") %>'
>
    Hyperlink Label
</asp:HyperLink>
```

220: What is the easiest way to bring down any website?

Answer:

A website can be shut down by creating an html file named as App_offline.htm. The file should be deployed in the application root directory. The .NET runtime handles the internal runtimes. When the .NET framework finds the file in the root directory it shuts down the application domain for the application. It responds with the contents of the App_offline.htm for any dynamic request. To make the site up and running again, the file has to be deleted from the root folder.

221: How to print out all the variables in the Session?

Answer:

Session.Keys can be used to get all the session variables
The following code gives all the session variables

```
foreach (string strSessionVar in Session.Keys)
{
Response.Write(strSessionVar + " : " +
Session[strSessionVar].ToString() + "<br>");

}
```

222: What are the security threats for any website?

Answer:

The following are the main security threats that need to be handled:

a) SQL Injection

b) Cross side scripting

c) Storing password without encoding

d) Input forms without validations

223: What are different ways with which hacking can be prevented?

Answer:

a) **Authentication/Authorization**: Setting registration and login and giving rights to the user based on role

b) **Encryption/Decryption**: Securing key inputs such as passwords

c) **Maintaining web servers outside Corporate Firewall**: Protection from hacks through firewalls

224: Name few built in permission-sets in .NET.

Answer:

The following are some of the permission-sets available in .NET framework:

a) FullTrust

b) Execution

c) LocalInternet

d) Internet

e) Nothing

225: What are the attributes available in <httpRuntime> node?

Answer:

The web.config file has the node <httpRuntime> which has several attributes.

<httpRuntime

executionTimeout="100" maxRequestLength="2048"

requestLengthDiskThreshold="80"

useFullyQualifiedRedirectUrl="false"

minFreeThreads="9" minLocalRequestFreeThreads="4"

appRequestQueueLimit="5050"

enableKernelOutputCache="true"

enableVersionHeader="false"

requireRootedSaveAsPath="false"

enable="true" shutdownTimeout="60"

delayNotificationTimeout="5"

waitChangeNotification="1"

maxWaitChangeNotification="1"

enableHeaderChecking="true"

sendCacheControlHeader="false"

apartmentThreading="false" />

226: Give the code snippet of config file.

Answer:

The following is the sample code snippet of a config file

<configuration>

    <system.diagnostics>

        <switches>

            <add name="MyField" value="10" />

```
        </switches>
      </system.diagnostics>
</configuration>
```

227: What is the use of @Page Directive?

Answer:

@Page Directive can be used to specify attributes that may affect the page in the .aspx page.

```
<%@Page Language="C#" Debug="true" %>
<%@ Page attribute="myvalue" [attribute="myvalue"...] %>
```

228: Explain about the readystate property.

Answer:

Readystate is a property which holds the responses from server generated based on the request from client side. Some of the values of ReadyState property are:

If status is 0, request is not initialized

For status=1, the request is set up

Status=2, request is sent

Status=3, request is in process

Status=4, request is complete.

229: List the new features of ASP.NET 4 web forms.

Answer:

Some of the features of ASP.NET 4 are:

a) Ability to set Metatags

b) Routing

c) More control over the ViewState

d) Ability to persist the selected rows in data control

e) Filtering support for datasource controls

This page is intentionally left blank.

Chapter 7

Remoting and Webservices

230: Explain in brief about remoting in .net. List the different components of the remoting framework.

Answer:

The remoting in .net provides communication between the various application domains through the remoting framework. The location can be computers in the same network, or on different networks. The TCP and HTTP channels are used for data communication.

The main components of the remoting framework are:

a) **C# Remote Listener:** The C# remote listener is used for listening to the requests for the remote object in an application.

b) **C# Remote Formatters:** The use of formatters in .net is for decoding and encoding the data before it is transferred through the channel. The SOAP formatter and binary formatter are used for formatting.

c) **C# Remote Activation:** The activation of the remote objects can be client or server side. The objects of server side are not created when they are instantiated by the client. They are created only when they are needed in the functionality.

d) **C# Remoting Channels:** The use of remoting channels is to transfer the data to the remote objects and receive from them. They are implemented using the configuration file or through the ChannelServices.RegisterChannel. The HTTP channel transfers the message to and from the remote objects. SOAP protocol is used. The TCP channel uses the binary formatter for message transfer.

231:What criteria from communication options can be selected in a distributed application technology?

Answer:

There are various ways used for communication with the application domain objects in C#. The inter process communication, integration and the business needs are used for programming model selection.

The different criteria used for communication in a distributed application are as listed below:

a) **Interoperability:** It is necessary for the application to interoperate among the different operating systems. The .net framework provides user with the flexibility to work on different platforms.

b) **Scalability:** It is easy for the user to host the application in the IIS. It provides user with the flexibility.

c) **CLR features:** The .net clients are widely used by the services and .net remoting. The features of .net can be used which are not available for the web service created by the user. The features like indexers, properties, callcontext, etc can be used.

d) **Communication across different domains:** The communication between the application domain and objects is possible through remoting.

e) **Object oriented features:** The object oriented features like references to remote object, state management, object activation options are supported by remoting.

232: What is a web service? What are the different ways for web service development?

Answer:

The functionality dependent on web used for accessing the web protocols and can be used in the web applications. There are three different ways for accessing the web service development as listed below:

a) **Web service creation:** The web service is defined by a web application containing the class with different methods used by different applications. User can declare the methods containing different parameters in the web service creation.

b) **Web service consumption:** The web service can be easily consumed by creating a new web site in the same solution hierarchy. The web page must contain the controls corresponding to the methods.

c) **Proxy creation:** A proxy is always created and registered with the client application. It handles the calls made by the client application, adds in a proper format and using the SOAP protocol the request is sent to the server. The messages are exchanged using the SOAP protocol. The message sent by the client are decoded and returned to the client application.

233: Create a web service to define the multiplication of three numbers in C#.

Answer:

The steps for creating the web service defining the multiplication of three numbers are:

a) Open the visual studio application in your system. Create ASP.NET web service under the templates option

b) Add a name to the web service and switch to the code view window

c) Add the code to the new created web service class
```
[WebMethod]
public int multiplication ( int x, int y, int  z)
{
    return x * y * z;
}
```

d) Build the application by clicking on the build option

e) For consuming the service, select C# projects and click the console application

f) From the Project menu, click Add Web Reference option

g) Add the address of the service in the address textbox and hit enter

h) In the Main method, add the following code for creating the proxy object

localhost.Service1 multiservice= new localhost.Service1();

i) Invoke method on the object created by the user

Console.WriteLine("Multiplication is: 3 * 4 * 5 = {0}, multiservice.multiplication (3,4,5));

j) Build and debug the application and output is displayed on the console window

234: What is .NET Remoting?

Answer:

The technology through which communication between different application domains is achieved is .NET Remoting. To provide communication between a client application and a server application can be achieved using different technologies. HTTP and TCP channels can be used.

The objects of .NET remoting should be tightly coupled as communication occurs between different domains. XML can be used for web services to send message across the network. Using Formatter class, messages are serialized.

235: What are two ways of creating remoting objects?

Answer:

Objects can be created in two ways using remoting and they are:

a) **SAO (Server Activated Objects):** It follows two modes namely "single call" and "singleton"

b) **CAO (Client Activated Objects):** It is stateful as compared to SAO. The creation request is raised from the client side

236: What is web service?

Answer:

Web service is a method of calling remote methods using HTTP using SOAP or REST. Web services can be described using the WSDL which allows discovering the web services dynamically at run time.

SOAP uses XML based standards and methods can be called using HTTP and the SOAP server can understand the incoming method request and returns standard format as response.

237: List out the components of web service.

Answer:

The components of web service are:

a) **ASMX File:** Web service extension file
b) **DISCO:** Discovery of Web service
c) **WSDL:** Web Services Description Language
d) **UDDI:** Universal Description, Discovery and Integration
e) **SOAP:** Simplified Object Access Protocol

238: What is SOAP?

Answer:

SOAP is a short form of Simplified Object Access Protocol. SOAP is a protocol which uses HTTP for processing remote service calls and returns details in XML Format.

SOAP is platform independent and consumer is shielded from the implementation details about the platform. As mentioned, as it is platform independent, a SOAP service deployed in windows environment can be accessed using UNIX and Linux platform.

239: What is WSDL?

Answer:

WSDL is the short form of Web Services Description Language. WSDL describes the web services, the available methods, and the various ways of calling the available methods and their types.

A typical WSDL looks like the below code

```
<?xml version="1.0" encoding="utf-8"?>

<definitions xmlns:soap="URL OF SOAP SCHEMA"
xmlns:http="URL OF HTTP SCHEMA" xmlns:s="URL OF
XML SCHEMA" xmlns:wsdl="URL OF WSDL SCHEMA" ...etc
namespaces...>

    <wsdl:types>

        <s:schema elementFormDefault="testqualified"
        targetNamespace="http://temporaryuri.org/">

        </s:schema>
    </wsdl:types>


...etc definitions...


</definitions>
```

240: What is DISCO?

Answer:

DISCO is the short form of Discovery of Web service and as the name specifies its functionality is to helps locate the web service. It contains the path where web service is installed.

It can be used to group common services on a web server and it provides links to the schema document of the web service.

241: What are the elements that should be contained in SOAP message?

Answer:

The following elements should be contained in SOAP message:

a) **Envelope Element:** It helps for XML documentation identification and translated it into a SOAP

b) **Header Element:** Header message is set in this element

c) **Body Element:** Call and Response messages are available in body element

d) **Fault Element:** Error occurred are handled by fault element

242: List the elements that need to be described in WSDL for SOAP.

Answer:

The following are xml elements required for SOAP and HTTP requests

```
<s:element name="DoResponse">
    <s:complexType>
        <s:sequence>
            <s:element minOccurs="2" maxOccurs="2"
            name="Result"
                type="s:int" />
        </s:sequence>
```

</s:complexType>
</s:element>

243: How can we make a method accessible through web service?

Answer:

The class file should use the following namespaces

    Using System;
    using System.Web;
    using System.Web.Services;
    using System.Web.Services.Protocols;

The below code states that webserivce class which should have be referenced in the asmx file.

    public class MyWebService :
    System.Web.Services.WebService{

        public MyWebService{
        }
    }

[webmethod] attribute should be mentioned in order to make a method to be accessible through web service

    [WebMethod]
    public string MyWebMethod()
    {
        return "My Result";
    }

244: How do we deploy a web service?

Answer:

   a) Web services can be deployed in IIS manually or through a project set up.

   b) Create a Virtual Directory in IIS. Map the directory to a project folder in the system drive

   c) The project folder should have the bin folder, web.config file of the web service and .asmx file

This service can be accessed through browser like

http://<system ip address where the service is

available>/<name of virtual directory>/<file name>.asmx

245: How to consume a web service?

Answer:

The following code should be written in a .cs file of a project

```
MyWebService objWebService = new MyWebService();
string Myresult = objWebService.MyWebMethod();
```

Use the following code for Default.aspx file

```
<form id="form1" runat="server">
    <div>
        <asp:Label Runat="server" ID="resultSection" />
        <br />
        <asp:Button Runat="server" ID="EnableButton"
        Text="Invoke MyWebMethod()"
        OnClick="EnableButton_Click" />
    </div>
</form>
```

Add a reference to the web service to the project and write the below code in default.aspx.cs file.

```
protected void EnableButton_Click(object objsender,
EventArgs e)
{
    MyWebService ObjService = new MyWebService();
    resultSection.Text = ObjService.MyWebMethod();
}
```

246: What are the data types supported in web services?
Answer:

.NET web services follows SOAP standards which use XML based standards to exchange data and so the web services can support data types that are recognized by XML schema standard. FileStream, Eventlog type of .NET objects are not universally recognized are not supported by web services.

Dataset and DataTable can be used to return information and ADO.NET objects like DataColumns and DataRows cannot be used.

247: What are the common collection types used in C#?
Answer:

Collection types can vary, depending on how the elements are stored, sorted, how searches are performed and how comparisons are made. The most common collection types in C# are: List<T>: Represents a strongly typed list of objects that can be accessed by index. It provides methods to search, sort and manipulate lists and Dictionary<TKey, TValue>: Represents a collection of keys and values.

Some other useful collections include Array, ArrayList, Queue (First-In-First-Out logic), Stack (Last-In-First-Out logic).

248: What the different phase/steps of acquiring a proxy object in Web service?

Answer:

Following are the different phases/steps of acquiring a proxy object in Web service:

a) The client communicates to the UDI for web service. The request is raised through UDDI's public web service or through browser

b) UDII responds with a list of web service

c) Each web service will have a URI pointing to a WSDL document

d) The client parses the WSDL document and it builds a proxy object

249: How to call a web service hosted in multiple servers dynamically during run time?

Answer:

The WSDL will be generated when a web service is added to the client. WSDL has the URL of the web service and so the web reference is associated with single URL

Before calling the web service changes the URL to URL where calling web service will be located.

```
string ws_path = "http://" + WSIpAddress + WebServiceURl;
    <WebserviceObject>.Url = ws_path;
```

250: What do you mean by SOAP encoding?

Answer:

SOAP message do not include default encoding. encodingStyle attribute can be used to define data types in the document. It can appear in any of the SOAP elements

Soap:encodingStyle="URI"

XML format is used for encoding data.

251: Why should we Encrypt SOAP messages?

Answer:

If messages are exchanged in plain text it has the possibility to be viewed by anyone in internet. SOAP over the HTTPS is secured. SOAP response messages with unencrypted data can be accessed easily.

The HTTP messages including the body of the http message and the header is encrypted with the help of public asymmetric encryption algorithms. By using SOAP encryption class, any specific part of SOAP message could be encrypted.

252: What is the difference between .NET remoting and web services?

Answer:

a) Web services can be accessed only through HTTP where remoting can be accessed by any protocol like TCP, HTTP and SMTP.

b) When remoting is used by TCP with binary format, performance is better compared to web services.

c) If remoting is hosted other than IIS location security aspect

should be taken care while web services are hosted in IIS
and IIS handles the security part.

d) Web services are platform independent where .NET
remoting can be accessed using an application developed
in .NET

e) Creation and consumption of web services are easier
better compared to remoting.

253: What is an application domain?

Answer:

Application isolation can be achieved by application domain.
Using this multiple applications can run within the same process
without interacting with the other application. If error occurs in
one application domain the other is not affected which continues
to run without problem. In order to invoke a method which is
available in a remote domain we go for remoting.

Using AppDomain class one can create and terminate application
domains.

254: Explain about contexts.

Answer:

Context is a boundary which contains collections of objects and is
similar to COM+ contexts. The application domain itself is
something similar to a sub process with security boundaries.
Application domain can have different contexts. Using contents,
objects of similar execution requirements can be grouped together.
Contexts are composed from set of properties and they are used
for interception.

255: What are remote objects?

Answer:

Distributed computing requires remote objects. Any object that needs to be called remotely must be derived from System.MarshalByRefObject namespace. It uses a proxy object to access the remote object.

A remote object has distributed identity and this allows a reference to be passed to other clients and they still continue to access the same object.

256: List the main elements and attributes of system.runtime.remoting.

Answer:

a) Using application element the name of the application can be specified using the name attribute.

b) Using service element we can specify a collection of remote objects. Service element has *wellknow* and *activated* sub elements.

c) Client element has a url attribute to specify the url to remote object.

d) Activated element can be used for client-activated objects.

257: How can we stop a thread?

Answer:

Thread class has support to instruct the thread to stop. There are two methods available in Thread class and they are Thread.Interrupt() and Thread.Abort()

a) **Thread.Interrupt** invokes ThreadInterruptedException on a thread when it goes into a WaitJoinSleep State.

b) **Thread.Abort** throws ThreadAbortException regardless of whatever the thread is working on.

258: How to perform tracing/logging?

Answer:

Debug and Trace are the two classes which deal with tracing. This can be done using the System.Diagnostics namespace. Use the System.Diagnostics.Trace.WriteLine namespace to trace during the debug and release builds.

System.Diagnostics.Debug.WriteLine namespace can be used to trace that we want to work only in debug builds.

259: How to redirect tracing to a file?

Answer:

Both Trace and Debug classes have a Listeners Property that receives the tracing which is sent through Debug.WriteLine and Trace.WriteLine. Listener collection has a single sink instance of DefaultTraceListner class.

The TextWriterTracerListener class helps for redirecting the output of Trace into file

```
Trace.Listeners.Clear();
FileStream objfs = new FileStream(@"D:\myfolder\MyLog.txt",
FM.Create, FA.Write );

Trace.Listeners.Add(new TextWriterTraceListener(objfs) );
Trace.WriteLine(@"Content to write to c:\myfolder\log.txt!");
Trace.Flush();
```

In the above code, FM denotes FileMode and FA denotes FileAccess.

260: Why strings are called immutable data types?

Answer:

The memory representation of string data type is an array of characters. When the re-assigning happens, a new array of char data type is formed and the start address is changed. In this case the previously occupied memory will be available for the Garbage collector for dispose functionality.

261: How to customize the serialization process?

Answer:

a) XMLSerializer supports lots of attributes which can be used for configuring serialization for any particular class.

b) [XmlIgnore] attribute can be used to exclude a field or property from serialization.

c) [XmlElement] attribute can be used to specify which XML element needs to be used for a particular field or property.

262: What is WebClient?

Answer:

a) .NET supports System.Net.WebClient namespace which can be used to download a file from a remote location and also to upload files to a remote location.

b) Webclient can download a file and also helps to read the file content.

c) URI with http:, https:, File: identifiers are supported by

WebClient.

263: How can we download files?

Answer:

WebClient provides two methods which can be used to download a file. DownloadFile() method can be used to download a file and store it in local storage. There are two parameters URI of the file and location where the file needs to be stored are available for the method.

```
WebClient Client = new WebClient();
Client.DownloadFile("http://www.reuters.com/",
"ReutersHomepage.htm");
```

264: How to read contents of a file or URI using WebClient?

Answer:

OpenRead method of WebClient can be used to display contents of a page.

```
public MyForm()
{
    InitializeComponent();
    System.Net.WebClient ObjClient = new WebClient();
    Stream Objstrm =
    Client.OpenRead("http://www.yourwebsite.com");
    StreamReader Objsr = new StreamReader(Objstrm);
    string content_line;
    while ( (content_line=Objsr.ReadLine()) != null )
    {
        MylistBox1.Items.Add(content_line);
    }
}
```

```
    Objstrm.Close();
}
```

265: How can we upload files using WebClient?

Answer:

Using UploadFile method a file can be uploaded to the given location. UploadData method can be used to transfer binary data to the specified URI.

```
WebClient Objclient = new WebClient();
Objclient.UploadFile("http://www.yourwebsite.com/filename.html",
"D:\\localfolder\\NewFile.html");
byte[] image; // code to initialise as binary data
// some jpg file
Objclient.UploadData("http://www.yourwebsite.com/filename.jpg", image);
```

266: What is Marshaling?

Answer:

When an object is converted in order to be sent across the network or across application domains Marshaling can be used. There are two ways of Marshaling available and they are:

a) **Marshal-by-value:** Object is serialized and copy of the object will be created on the other of network

b) **Marshaling-by-reference:** Proxy is created on the client that can be used to communicate with the client Objects derived using MarshalByRefObject are marshaled by reference

267: What is ObjRef object in Remoting?

Answer:

All Marshal Methods return the ObjRef object. ObjRef implements the ISerializable interface and it can be marshaled by value. The ObjRef is aware of:

a) The location of the remote object

b) Port Number

c) Host Name

d) Object Name

268: How can we do windows authentication for web services?

Answer:

The following are the steps to be followed for achieving this -

a) In the web.config file change the authentication mode element to "Windows" in the web service.

        \<authentication mode="Windows" /\>

b) Before calling any method of the web service set the credentials property on the client side.

        \<webserviceName\>.Credentials = new System.Net.NetworkCredential(UserName, Password);

c) Disable the Anonymous Authentication and then enable the Windows Authentication in the IIS Admin.

269: Define declarative and imperative security.

Answer:

Declarative security can be applied on classes and methods by associating attribute declarations that can specify and security action.

By calling appropriate methods of Permission object that represents system resource is done by Imperative security. The security constraints are stored in assembly during compile time.

270: What is DLL Hell?

Answer:

DLL Hell arises when a new version of application and a new version of DLL override the old version.

The application which points to the older version of the DLL get crashed as the new DLL is installed in place of old DLL. The functions used in old DLL and which are not supported in new DLL are not compatible for the current version and it crash the application.

271: What is a PE file?

Answer:

PE is the short form of Portable Executable. A PE file can be a DLL or EXE. A PE file is created when a program is compiled.

The PE file consists of three sections:

- a) PE Header
- b) MSIL
- c) MetaData

272: How public key cryptography works?

Answer:

In Cryptography both sender and the receiver will have keys which are known as public keys with which assembly can be encrypted. Both sender and receiver will have a private key using which the assembly can be decrypted.

During sign of an assembly both public and private keys are embedded into the assembly. The consumer of the assembly will be provided with the private key.

273: Explain about refactoring of web.config.

Answer:

Most of the configuration elements are moved to machine.config in ASP.NET version 4.0.

Using this, the version of .Net Framework targeted by the application can be mentioned as stated below:

```
< ? xml version="1.0" ? >
<configuration1>
    <system.web>
        <compilation targetFramework = "4.0" />
    </system.web>
</configuration1>
```

274: What is Forms Authentication ticket?

Answer:

Cookies which are stored when a user is authenticated which are stored in client machine are called Forms Authentication ticket.

This helps user to automatically login into the application when the user revisits the website.

The Ticket information will be sent to web server with the HTTP request when the user revisits the site.

275: What are the features of ASP.NET 4.0?

Answer:

Following are the features of ASP.NET 4.0:

a) Compression of Session state

b) Routing in ASP.NET

c) HTML Encode New syntax

d) Extensible output cache

e) Individual view control state mode

f) New properties like Page.MetaKeyword and Page.MetaDescription

g) New method Response.RedirectPermenant

h) Improvements on Microsoft Ajax Library

i) Refactoring of web.config file

j) Auto-start of ASP.NET applications

k) Increase of URL character length

276: Define the term channel in .NET remoting.

Answer:

In remoting, an application uses channel to send any message to another application which might be running in different domain or a process. Before sending the actual message, Channel converts messages into XML or binary format. The Channel which carries the message can use HTTP and TCP protocol.

Channel can be HTTP or TCP. HTTPChannel uses SoapFormatter to serialize the messages into the XML document. The TCPChannel uses binaryformatter to serialize all the messages into binary stream.

277: What are remotable and non-remotable objects in Remoting?

Answer:

Objects that can be distributed across application domains, can be used with the domain are named as remotable.

Objects that cannot be distributed across domains are names as non-remotable. In any distributed system, if any object is bigger, it can be set to non-remotable object.

278: List the different type of collections available in .NET.

Answer:

Collections are group of records which are treated as one logical unit. There are four categories of collection available and they are:

a) Indexed Based
b) Key Value pair
c) Specialized collection
d) Prioritized Collection

279: What is Generic?

Answer:

Using generics we can create flexible strong type collections. It separates the logic from the datatype to maintain better reusability and maintainability. To implement generic import the System.Collections.Generic namespace.

When a class or method is set with unknown datatype, method which has arguments set to unknown datatype and when method is called using an object any similar content type of data can be passed as argument.

280: What are special collections?

Answer:

These are tailored .net collection meant for specific purposes.

There are many types of collection available .NET and some of them are:

  a) CollectionsUtil
  b) ListCollection
  c) HybridCollection
  d) StringCollection

281: Explain about CollectionsUtil.

Answer:

It helps to create collection that ignores the strings in case.

```
Hashtable ObjMyHash =
CollectionsUtil.CreateCaseInsensitiveHashtable();

ObjMyHash.Add("some STRING","empty content");
string objstr = (string) ObjHash["SOME STRING"];
MessageBox.Show(objstr);
```

282: Explain about ListCollection.

Answer:

This can be used where a collection has less number of characters.

```
ListDictionary ObjMyDic = new ListDictionary();
ObjMyDic.Add("TEST", "my test string");
ObjMyDic.Add("NEW", "my test string");
```

283: What are the different types of Generic collection?

Answer:

There are four different types of generic collections available and they are:

a) **List:** These are index based generic collections

b) **Dictionary:** Key based

c) **Stack:** Allows getting values in LIFO manner

d) **Queue:** Allows getting values in FIFO manner

284: How to use dictionary class?

Answer:

First create a dictionary object. Populate the dictionary class enumerate it in order to display key value pairs.

In order to have integer as key and strings as values we have to create dictionary of following format.

```
ObjdicNames.Add(1,"Value1");
ObjdicNames.Add(3,"Value2");
ObjdicNames.Add(5,"Value3");
```

HR Questions

Review these typical interview questions and think about how you would answer them. Read the answers listed; you will find best possible answers along with strategies and suggestions.

1: Tell me about a time when you worked additional hours to finish a project.

Answer:

It's important for your employer to see that you are dedicated to your work, and willing to put in extra hours when required or when a job calls for it. However, be careful when explaining why you were called to work additional hours – for instance, did you have to stay late because you set goals poorly earlier in the process? Or on a more positive note, were you working additional hours because a client requested for a deadline to be moved up on short notice? Stress your competence and willingness to give 110% every time.

2: Tell me about a time when your performance exceeded the duties and requirements of your job.

Answer:

If you're a great candidate for the position, this should be an easy question to answer – choose a time when you truly went above and beyond the call of duty, and put in additional work or voluntarily took on new responsibilities. Remain humble, and express gratitude for the learning opportunity, as well as confidence in your ability to give a repeat performance.

3: What is your driving attitude about work?

Answer:

There are many possible good answers to this question, and the interviewer primarily wants to see that you have a great passion for the job and that you will remain motivated in your career if hired. Some specific driving forces behind your success may include hard work, opportunity, growth potential, or success.

4: Do you take work home with you?

Answer:

It is important to first clarify that you are always willing to take work home when necessary, but you want to emphasize as well that it has not been an issue for you in the past. Highlight skills such as time management, goal-setting, and multi-tasking, which can all ensure that work is completed at work.

5: Describe a typical work day to me.

Answer:

There are several important components in your typical work day, and an interviewer may derive meaning from any or all of them, as well as from your ability to systematically lead him or her through the day. Start at the beginning of your day and proceed chronologically, making sure to emphasize steady productivity, time for review, goal-setting, and prioritizing, as well as some additional time to account for unexpected things that may arise.

6: Tell me about a time when you went out of your way at your previous job.

Answer:

Here it is best to use a specific example of the situation that required you to go out of your way, what your specific position would have required that you did, and how you went above that. Use concrete details, and be sure to include the results, as well as reflection on what you learned in the process.

7: Are you open to receiving feedback and criticisms on your job performance, and adjusting as necessary?

Answer:

This question has a pretty clear answer – yes – but you'll need to display a knowledge as to why this is important. Receiving feedback and criticism is one thing, but the most important part of that process is to then implement it into your daily work. Keep a good attitude, and express that you always appreciate constructive feedback.

8: What inspires you?

Answer:

You may find inspiration in nature, reading success stories, or mastering a difficult task, but it's important that your inspiration is positively-based and that you're able to listen and tune into it when it appears. Keep this answer generally based in the professional world, but where applicable, it may stretch a bit into creative exercises in your personal life that, in turn, help you in achieving career objectives.

9: How do you inspire others?

Answer:

This may be a difficult question, as it is often hard to discern the effects of inspiration in others. Instead of offering a specific example of a time when you inspired someone, focus on general principles such as leading by example that you employ in your professional life. If possible, relate this to a quality that someone who inspired you possessed, and discuss the way you have modified or modeled it in your own work.

10: What has been your biggest success?
Answer:

Your biggest success should be something that was especially meaningful to you, and that you can talk about passionately – your interviewer will be able to see this. Always have an answer prepared for this question, and be sure to explain how you achieved success, as well as what you learned from the experience.

11: What motivates you?
Answer:

It's best to focus on a key aspect of your work that you can target as a "driving force" behind your everyday work. Whether it's customer service, making a difference, or the chance to further your skills and gain experience, it's important that the interviewer can see the passion you hold for your career and the dedication you have to the position.

12: What do you do when you lose motivation?
Answer:

The best candidates will answer that they rarely lose motivation, because they already employ strategies to keep themselves inspired, and because they remain dedicated to their objectives. Additionally, you may impress the interviewer by explaining that

you are motivated by achieving goals and advancing, so small
successes are always a great way to regain momentum.

13: What do you like to do in your free time?
Answer:

What you do answer here is not nearly as important as what you
don't answer – your interviewer does not want to hear that you
like to drink, party, or revel in the nightlife. Instead, choose a few
activities to focus on that are greater signs of stability and
maturity, and that will not detract from your ability to show up to
work and be productive, such as reading, cooking, or
photography. This is also a great opportunity to show your
interviewer that you are a well-rounded, interesting, and dynamic
personality that they would be happy to hire.

14: What sets you apart from other workers?
Answer:

This question is a great opportunity to highlight the specific skill
sets and passion you bring to the company that no one else can. If
you can't outline exactly what sets you apart from other workers,
how will the interviewer see it? Be prepared with a thorough
outline of what you will bring to the table, in order to help the
company achieve their goals.

15: Why are you the best candidate for that position?
Answer:

Have a brief response prepared in advance for this question, as
this is another very common theme in interviews (variations of the

question include: "Why should I hire you, above Candidate B?" and "What can you bring to our company that Candidate B cannot?"). Make sure that your statement does not sound rehearsed, and highlight your most unique qualities that show the interviewer why he or she must hire you above all the other candidates. Include specific details about your experience and special projects or recognition you've received that set you apart, and show your greatest passion, commitment, and enthusiasm for the position.

16: What does it take to be successful?
Answer:

Hard work, passion, motivation, and a dedication to learning – these are all potential answers to the ambiguous concept of success. It doesn't matter so much which of these values you choose as the primary means to success, or if you choose a combination of them. It is, however, absolutely key that whichever value you choose, you must clearly display in your attitude, experience, and goals.

17: What would be the biggest challenge in this position for you?
Answer:

Keep this answer positive, and remain focused on the opportunities for growth and learning that the position can provide. Be sure that no matter what the challenge is, it's obvious that you're ready and enthusiastic to tackle it, and that you have a full awareness of what it will take to get the job done.

18: Would you describe yourself as an introvert or an extrovert?

Answer:

There are beneficial qualities to each of these, and your answer may depend on what type of work you're involved in. However, a successful leader may be an introvert or extrovert, and similarly, solid team members may also be either. The important aspect of this question is to have the level of self-awareness required to accurately describe yourself.

19: What are some positive character traits that you don't possess?

Answer:

If an interviewer asks you a tough question about your weaknesses, or lack of positive traits, it's best to keep your answer light-hearted and simple – for instance, express your great confidence in your own abilities, followed by a (rather humble) admittance that you could occasionally do to be more humble.

20: What is the greatest lesson you've ever learned?

Answer:

While this is a very broad question, the interviewer will be more interested in hearing what kind of emphasis you place on this value. Your greatest lesson may tie in with something a mentor, parent, or professor once told you, or you may have gleaned it from a book written by a leading expert in your field. Regardless of what the lesson is, it is most important that you can offer an example of how you've incorporated it into your life.

21: Have you ever been in a situation where one of your strengths became a weakness in an alternate setting?

Answer:

It's important to show an awareness of yourself by having an answer for this question, but you want to make sure that the weakness is relatively minor, and that it would still remain a strength in most settings. For instance, you may be an avid reader who reads anything and everything you can find, but reading billboards while driving to work may be a dangerous idea.

22: Who has been the most influential person in your life?

Answer:

Give a specific example (and name) to the person who has influenced your life greatly, and offer a relevant anecdote about a meaningful exchange the two of you shared. It's great if their influence relates to your professional life, but this particular question opens up the possibility to discuss inspiration in your personal life as well. The interviewer wants to see that you're able to make strong connections with other individuals, and to work under the guiding influence of another person.

23: Do you consider yourself to be a "detailed" or "big picture" type of person?

Answer:

Both of these are great qualities, and it's best if you can incorporate each into your answer. Choose one as your primary type, and relate it to experience or specific items from your resume. Then, explain how the other type fits into your work as well.

24: What is your greatest fear?

Answer:

Disclosing your greatest fear openly and without embarrassment is a great way to show your confidence to an employer. Choose a fear that you are clearly doing work to combat, such as a fear of failure that will seem impossible to the interviewer for someone such as yourself, with such clear goals and actions plans outlined. As tempting as it may be to stick with an easy answer such as spiders, stay away from these, as they don't really tell the interviewer anything about yourself that's relevant.

25: What sort of challenges do you enjoy?

Answer:

The challenges you enjoy should demonstrate some sort of initiative or growth potential on your part, and should also be in line with your career objectives. Employers will evaluate consistency here, as they analyze critically how the challenges you look forward to are related to your ultimate goals.

26: Tell me about a time you were embarrassed. How did you handle it?

Answer:

No one wants to bring up times they were embarrassed in a job interview, and it's probably best to avoid an anecdote here. However, don't shy away from offering a brief synopsis, followed by a display of your ability to laugh it off. Show the interviewer that it was not an event that impacted you significantly.

27: What is your greatest weakness?

Answer:

This is another one of the most popular questions asked in job interviews, so you should be prepared with an answer already. Try to come up with a weakness that you have that can actually be a strength in an alternate setting – such as, "I'm very detail-oriented and like to ensure that things are done correctly, so I sometimes have difficulty in delegating tasks to others." However, don't try to mask obvious weaknesses – if you have little practical experience in the field, mention that you're looking forward to great opportunities to further your knowledge.

28: What are the three best adjectives to describe you in a work setting?

Answer:

While these three adjectives probably already appear somewhere on your resume, don't be afraid to use them again in order to highlight your best qualities. This is a chance for you to sell yourself to the interviewer, and to point out traits you possess that other candidates do not. Use the most specific and accurate words you can think of, and elaborate shortly on how you embody each.

29: What are the three best adjectives to describe you in your personal life?

Answer:

Ideally, the three adjectives that describe you in your personal life should be similar to the adjectives that describe you in your professional life. Employers appreciate consistency, and while they may be understanding of you having an alternate personality outside of the office, it's best if you employ similar principles in your actions both on and off the clock.

30: What type of worker are you?

Answer:

This is an opportunity for you to highlight some of your greatest assets. Characterize some of your talents such as dedicated, self-motivated, detail-oriented, passionate, hard-working, analytical, or customer service focused. Stay away from your weaker qualities here, and remain on the target of all the wonderful things that you can bring to the company.

31: Tell me about your happiest day at work.

Answer:

Your happiest day at work should include one of your greatest professional successes, and how it made you feel. Stay focused on what you accomplished, and be sure to elaborate on how rewarding or satisfying the achievement was for you.

32: Tell me about your worst day at work.

Answer:

It may have been the worst day ever because of all the mistakes you made, or because you'd just had a huge argument with your best friend, but make sure to keep this answer professionally focused. Try to use an example in which something uncontrollable happened in the workplace (such as an important member of a team quit unexpectedly, which ruined your team's meeting with a client), and focus on the frustration of not being in control of the situation. Keep this answer brief, and be sure to end with a reflection on what you learned from the day.

33: What are you passionate about?

Answer:

Keep this answer professionally-focused where possible, but it may also be appropriate to discuss personal issues you are passionate about as well (such as the environment or volunteering at a soup kitchen). Stick to issues that are non-controversial, and allow your passion to shine through as you explain what inspires you about the topic and how you stay actively engaged in it. Additionally, if you choose a personal passion, make sure it is one that does not detract from your availability to work or to be productive.

34: What is the piece of criticism you receive most often?

Answer:

An honest, candid answer to this question can greatly impress an interviewer (when, of course, it is coupled with an explanation of what you're doing to improve), but make sure the criticism is something minimal or unrelated to your career.

35: What type of work environment do you succeed the most in?

Answer:

Be sure to research the company and the specific position before heading into the interview. Tailor your response to fit the job you'd be working in, and explain why you enjoy that type of environment over others. However, it's also extremely important to be adaptable, so remain flexible to other environments as well.

36: Are you an emotional person?

Answer:

It's best to focus on your positive emotions – passion, happiness, motivations – and to stay away from other extreme emotions that may cause you to appear unbalanced. While you want to display your excitement for the job, be sure to remain level-headed and cool at all times, so that the interviewer knows you're not the type of person who lets emotions take you over and get in the way of your work.

37: Tell me about your favorite book or newspaper.

Answer:

The interviewer will look at your answer to this question in order to determine your ability to analyze and review critically. Additionally, try to choose something that is on a topic related to your field or that embodies a theme important to your work, and be able to explain how it relates. Stay away from controversial subject matter, such as politics or religion.

38: If you could be rich or famous, which would you choose?

Answer:

This question speaks to your ability to think creatively, but your answer may also give great insight to your character. If you answer rich, your interviewer may interpret that you are self-confident and don't seek approval from others, and that you like to be rewarded for your work. If you choose famous, your interviewer may gather that you like to be well-known and to deal with people, and to have the platform to deliver your message to others. Either way, it's important to back up your answer with sound reasoning.

39: If you could trade places with anyone for a week, who would it be and why?

Answer:

This question is largely designed to test your ability to think on your feet, and to come up with a reasonable answer to an outside the box question. Whoever you choose, explain your answer in a logical manner, and offer specific professional reasons that led you to choose the individual.

40: What would you say if I told you that just from glancing over your resume, I can already see three spelling mistakes?

Answer:

Clearly, your resume should be absolutely spotless – and you should be confident that it is. If your interviewer tries to make you second-guess yourself here, remain calm and poised and assert with a polite smile that you would be quite surprised as you are positive that your resume is error-free.

41: Tell me about your worldview.

Answer:

This question is designed to offer insight into your personality, so be aware of how the interviewer will interpret your answer. Speak openly and directly, and try to incorporate your own job skills into your outlook on life. For example, discuss your beliefs on the ways that hard work and dedication can always bring success, or in how learning new things is one of life's greatest gifts. It's okay to expand into general life principles here, but try to keep your thoughts related to the professional field as well.

42: What is the biggest mistake someone could make in an interview?

Answer:

The biggest mistake that could be made in an interview is to be caught off guard! Make sure that you don't commit whatever you answer here, and additionally be prepared for all questions. Other common mistakes include asking too early in the hiring process about job benefits, not having questions prepared when the interviewer asks if you have questions, arriving late, dressing casually or sloppily, or showing ignorance of the position.

43: If you won the $50m lottery, what would you do with the money?

Answer:

While a question such as this may seem out of place in a job interview, it's important to display your creative thinking and your ability to think on the spot. It's also helpful if you choose something admirable, yet believable, to do with the money such as donate the first seventy percent to a charitable cause, and divide the remainder among gifts for friends, family, and of course, yourself.

44: Is there ever a time when honesty isn't appropriate in the workplace?

Answer:

This may be a difficult question, but the only time that honesty isn't appropriate in the workplace is perhaps when you're feeling anger or another emotion that is best kept to yourself. If this is the case, explain simply that it is best to put some thoughts aside, and clarify that the process of keeping some thoughts quiet is often enough to smooth over any unsettled emotions, thus eliminating the problem.

45: If you could travel anywhere in the world, where would it be?

Answer:

This question is meant to allow you to be creative – so go ahead and stretch your thoughts to come up with a unique answer. However, be sure to keep your answer professionally-minded. For example, choose somewhere rich with culture or that would expose you to a new experience, rather than going on an expensive cruise through the Bahamas.

46: What would I find in your refrigerator right now?

Answer:

An interviewer may ask a creative question such as this in order to discern your ability to answer unexpected questions calmly, or, to try to gain some insight into your personality. For example, candidates with a refrigerator full of junk food or take-out may be more likely to be under stress or have health issues, while a candidate with a balanced refrigerator full of nutritious staples may be more likely to lead a balanced mental life, as well.

47: If you could play any sport professionally, what would it be and what aspect draws you to it?

Answer:

Even if you don't know much about professional sports, this question might be a great opportunity to highlight some of your greatest professional working skills. For example, you may choose to play professional basketball, because you admire the teamwork and coordination that goes into creating a solid play. Or, you may choose to play professional tennis, because you consider yourself to be a go-getter with a solid work ethic and great dedication to perfecting your craft. Explain your choice simply to the interviewer without elaborating on drawn-out sports metaphors, and be sure to point out specific areas or skills in which you excel.

48: Who were the presidential and vice-presidential candidates in the 2008 elections?

Answer:

This question, plain and simple, is intended as a gauge of your intelligence and awareness. If you miss this question, you may well fail the interview. Offer your response with a polite smile, because you understand that there are some individuals who probably miss this question.

49: Explain X task in a few short sentences as you would to a second-grader.

Answer:

An interviewer may ask you to break down a normal job task that you would complete in a manner that a child could understand, in part to test your knowledge of the task's inner workings – but in larger part, to test your ability to explain a process in simple, basic terms. While you and your coworkers may be able to converse using highly technical language, being able to simplify a process is an important skill for any employee to have.

50: If you could compare yourself to any animal, what would it be?

Answer:

Many interviewers ask this question, and it's not to determine which character traits you think you embody – instead, the interviewer wants to see that you can think outside the box, and that you're able to reason your way through any situation. Regardless of what animal you answer, be sure that you provide a thorough reason for your choice.

51: Who is your hero?

Answer:

Your hero may be your mother or father, an old professor, someone successful in your field, or perhaps even Wonder

Woman – but keep your reasoning for your choice professional, and be prepared to offer a logical train of thought. Choose someone who embodies values that are important in your chosen career field, and answer the question with a smile and sense of passion.

52: Who would play you in the movie about your life?

Answer:

As with many creative questions that challenge an interviewee to think outside the box, the answer to this question is not as important as how you answer it. Choose a professional, and relatively non-controversial actor or actress, and then be prepared to offer specific reasoning for your choice, employing important skills or traits you possess.

53: Name five people, alive or dead, that would be at your ideal dinner party.

Answer:

Smile and sound excited at the opportunity to think outside the box when asked this question, even if it seems to come from left field. Choose dynamic, inspiring individuals who you could truly learn from, and explain what each of them would have to offer to the conversation. Don't forget to include yourself, and to talk about what you would bring to the conversation as well!

54: What is customer service?

Answer:

Customer service can be many things – and the most important consideration in this question is that you have a creative answer. Demonstrate your ability to think outside the box by offering a confident answer that goes past a basic definition, and that shows you have truly considered your own individual view of what it means to take care of your customers. The thoughtful consideration you hold for customers will speak for itself.

55: Tell me about a time when you went out of your way for a customer.

Answer:

It's important that you offer an example of a time you truly went out of your way – be careful not to confuse something that felt like a big effort on your part, with something your employer would expect you to do anyway. Offer an example of the customer's problems, what you did to solve it, and the way the customer responded after you took care of the situation.

56: How do you gain confidence from customers?

Answer:

This is a very open-ended question that allows you to show your customer service skills to the interviewer. There are many possible answers, and it is best to choose something that you've had great experience with, such as "by handling situations with transparency," "offering rewards," or "focusing on great communication." Offer specific examples of successes you've had.

57: Tell me about a time when a customer was upset or agitated – how did you handle the situation?

Answer:

Similarly to handling a dispute with another employee, the most important part to answering this question is to first set up the scenario, offer a step-by-step guide to your particular conflict resolution style, and end by describing the way the conflict was resolved. Be sure that in answering questions about your own conflict resolution style, that you emphasize the importance of open communication and understanding from both parties, as well as a willingness to reach a compromise or other solution.

58: When can you make an exception for a customer?

Answer:

Exceptions for customers can generally be made when in accordance with company policy or when directed by a supervisor. Display an understanding of the types of situations in which an exception should be considered, such as when a customer has endured a particular hardship, had a complication with an order, or at a request.

59: What would you do in a situation where you were needed by both a customer and your boss?

Answer:

While both your customer and your boss have different needs of you and are very important to your success as a worker, it is always best to try to attend to your customer first – however, the key is explaining to your boss why you are needed urgently by the customer, and then to assure your boss that you will attend to his or her needs as soon as possible (unless it's absolutely an urgent matter).

60: What is the most important aspect of customer service?
Answer:

While many people would simply state that customer satisfaction is the most important aspect of customer service, it's important to be able to elaborate on other important techniques in customer service situations. Explain why customer service is such a key part of business, and be sure to expand on the aspect that you deem to be the most important in a way that is reasoned and well-thought out.

61: Is it best to create low or high expectations for a customer?
Answer:

You may answer this question either way (after, of course, determining that the company does not have a clear opinion on the matter). However, no matter which way you answer the question, you must display a thorough thought process, and very clear reasoning for the option you chose. Offer pros and cons of each, and include the ultimate point that tips the scale in favor of your chosen answer.

62: Why did you choose your college major?
Answer:

It's important to display interest in your work, and if your major is related to your current field, it will be simple for you to relate the two. Perhaps you even knew while in college that you wanted to do a job similar to this position, and so you chose the major so as to receive the education and training you needed to succeed. If your major doesn't relate clearly, it's still important to express a sense of passion for your choice, and to specify the importance of pursuing something that matters to you – which is how you made the decision to come to your current career field instead.

63 Tell me about your college experience.

Answer:

It's best to keep this answer positive – don't focus on parties, pizza, or procrastinating. Instead, offer a general summary of the benefits you received in college, followed by an anecdote of a favorite professor or course that opened up your way of thinking about the field you're in. This is a great opportunity for you to show your passion for your career, make sure to answer enthusiastically and confidently.

64: What is the most unique thing about yourself that you would bring to this position?

Answer:

This question is often asked as a close to an interview, and it gives you a final chance to highlight your best qualities to the employer. Treat the question like a sort of review, and explain why your specific mix of education, experience, and passions will be the ideal combination for the employer. Remain confident but humble, and keep your answer to about two minutes.

65: How did your last job stand up to your previous expectations of it?

Answer:

While it's okay to discuss what you learned if you expected too much out of a previous job, it's best to keep this question away from negative statements or portrayals. Focus your answer around what your previous job did hold that you had expected, and how much you enjoyed those aspects of the position.

66: How did you become interested in this field?

Answer:

This is the chance for you to show your passion for your career – and the interviewer will be assured that you are a great candidate if it's obvious that you enjoy your job. You can include a brief anecdote here in order to make your interest personal, but be sure that it is brief. Offer specific names of mentors or professors who aided in your discovery, and make it clear that you love what you do.

67: What was the greatest thing you learned while in school?

Answer:

By offering a lesson you learned outside of the classroom, you can show the interviewer your capacity for creativity, learning, and reflection. The practical lessons you learned in the classroom are certainly invaluable in their own right and may pertain closely to the position, but showing the mastery of a concept that you had to learn on your own will highlight your growth potential.

68: Tell me about a time when you had to learn a different skill set for a new position.

Answer:

Use a specific example to describe what you had to learn and how you set about outlining goals and tasks for yourself. It's important to show that you mastered the skill largely from your dedication to learning it, and because of the systematic approach you took to developing and honing your individual education. Additionally, draw connections between the skill you learned and the new position, and show how well prepared you are for the job.

69: Tell me about a person who has been a great influence in your career.

Answer:

It's important to make this answer easy to relate to – your story should remind the interviewer of the person who was most influential in his or her own career. Explain what you learned from this person and why they inspired you, and how you hope to model them later in your career with future successes.

70: What would this person tell me about you?

Answer:

Most importantly, if this person is one of your references –they had better know who you are! There are all too many horror stories of professors or past employers being called for a reference, and not being able to recall when they knew you or why you were remarkable, which doesn't send a very positive message to potential employers. This person should remember you as being enthusiastic, passionate, and motivated to learn and succeed.

71: What is the most productive time of day for you?

Answer:

This is a trick question – you should be equally productive all day! While it's normal to become extra motivated for certain projects, and also true that some tasks will require additional work, be sure to emphasize to the interviewer that working diligently throughout the entirety of the day comes naturally to you.

72: What was the most responsibility you were given at your previous job?

Answer:

This question provides you with an opportunity to elaborate on responsibilities that may or may not be on your resume. For instance, your resume may not have allowed room to discuss individual projects you worked on that were really outside the scope of your job responsibilities, but you can tell the interviewer here about the additional work you did and how it translated into new skills and a richer career experience for you.

73: Do you believe you were compensated fairly at your last job?

Answer:

Remember to stay positive, and to avoid making negative comments about your previous employer. If you were not compensated fairly, simply state that you believe your qualities and experience were outside the compensation limitations of the old job, and that you're looking forward to an opportunity that is more in line with the place you're at in your career.

74: Tell me about a time when you received feedback on your work, and enacted it.

Answer:

Try to give an example of feedback your received early in your career, and the steps you took to incorporate it with your work. The most important part of this question is to display the way you learned from the feedback, as well as your willingness to accept suggestions from your superiors. Be sure to offer reflection and understanding of how the feedback helped your work to improve.

75: Tell me about a time when you received feedback on your work that you did not agree with, or thought was unfair. How did you handle it?

Answer:

When explaining that you did not agree with particular feedback or felt it was unfair, you'll need to justify tactfully why the feedback was inaccurate. Then, explain how you communicated directly with the person who offered the feedback, and, most importantly, how you listened to their response, analyzed it, and then came to a mutual agreement.

76: What was your favorite job, and why?

Answer:

It's best if your favorite job relates to the position you're currently applying for, as you can then easily draw connections between why you enjoyed that job and why you are interested in the current position. Additionally, it is extremely important to explain why you've qualified the particular job as your favorite, and what aspects of it you would look for in another job, so that the interviewer can determine whether or not you are a good fit.

77: Tell me about an opportunity that your last position did not allow you to achieve.

Answer:

Stay focused on the positive, and be understanding of the limitations of your previous position. Give a specific example of a goal or career objective that you were not able to achieve, but rather than expressing disappointment over the missed opportunity, discuss the ways you're looking forward to the chance to grow in a new position.

78: Tell me about the worst boss you ever had.

Answer:

It's important to keep this answer brief, and positively focused. While you may offer a couple of short, critical assessments of your boss, focus on the things you learned from working with such an individual, and remain sympathetic to challenges the boss may have faced.

INDEX

C# Interview Questions

Introduction

22: What is a namespace?

23: Which is the base class of all classes in the .NET Framework? Please reference some methods of the class that can be overridden. What should you be aware of when using that class?

24: What is a Partial class?

25: What are static classes?

26: What are preprocessor directives?

27: List out the available preprocessor directives available in C#.

28: How do structs differ from class?

29: Can we create alias for namespaces?

Assemblies and Security

30: You are required to save the assemblies in a location where all the other computer applications can easily access them. Where should you add the assemblies?

31: There is a need to place the resource specific to a language in a different assembly. Which of the assemblies would help the user to add it?

32: Discuss the different security mechanisms used in .NET

33: What are the different components of code access security?

34: What are assemblies?

35: What is a private assembly?

36: What is a shared assembly?

37: What is a strong name?

38: What is a global assembly cache?

39: What is a Native Image Generator?

40: What is the use of a Global Assembly Cache Viewer?

41: What is a Gacutil?

42: How can we create a strong name?

43: How can we install a shared assembly?

44: What is delayed signing of assemblies?

45: How can you extract a public key and re-sign an assembly?

46: List out the types of settings available in configuration files.

47: What are the various version parts of an assembly?

48: What is Code Access Security?

49: List out various types of code group membership conditions.

50: What is CASPOL?

51: List various commands available in caspol.exe.

52: List out the code access permission provided by CLR.

53: What are the limitations of .NET security features?

54: How can you create and manage code groups?

55: What do you know about Thread Pooling? Describe its usage and how it can be used in C# applications.

56: What is threading?

57: List out the threadstate values.

58: What is the use of Threadpool?

59: What is locking?

Data Access

60: User needs to access the data from the student table using the DataReader object. What code should beadded for accessing the rows from the table?

61: What are the advantages of using the DataSet in a disconnected data structure

62: There are two tables as orderdetails and productdetails in the database. User needs to access the results from both the tables. What C# code must be added to access the data?

63: What are the different data adapter events used for responding to the changes made to the data source?

64: List the namespaces used for data access.

65: List out the classes available in System.Data namespace.

66: List out the Data Specific classes available in C.

Keywords

92: Which keywords can you use in order to specify how a method in a derived class interacts with a method with the same name in a base class?

93: What is the difference between Shadowing and Overriding?

94: Describe the *is* and as operators and their usage. (1.a – 4)

95: List the access modifiers available in C#.

96: Explain Protected Internal access modifier.

97: What is an internal access modifier?

98: What is a private access modifier?

99: What is a protected access modifier?

100: What is a public access modifier?

101: What is boxing?

102: What is unboxing?

103: Explain about the keyword Virtual.

104: Explain about Volatile keyword.

105: What are the restrictions for volatile keyword?

106:Explain about readonly keyword.

107: Describe the keywords used in C# for exception handling.

108:List out the constraints of override modifier.

109: What is the use of the keyword const?

110:What is the difference between readonly and const keywords?

111: Explain about the event keyword.

112: Explain the steps that need to be followed in order to create and use events.

113: Explain about implicit keyword.

114: Explain about explicit keyword.

115: What is side-by-side execution?

116: What is forward compatibility?

117: What is backward compatibility?

118: What is interoperability?

119: What is Friend Assemblies?

Windows Applications

120: What is use of event handling in windows forms. How can it be defined?

121: A windows form contains three textboxes for Name, Age and location. Define the code for the event handlers used for transferring the data in the read only boxes.

123: There is a textbox on the form which displays the value entered by the user. We need to validate the textbox using an event handler. Add the code for achieving the functionality.

124: List the various dialog control used in the Windows forms application.

125: How to create a Windows Form Application?

126: What are the user interaction keywords associated with events?

127: How can we create non rectangular window?

128: What are the form methods which control its lifecycle?

129: List out the user defined Data types.

130: Explain about the various configuration files.

131: List the debugging windows available.

132: What is the event of AddHandler Keyword?

133: How can we throw a custom exception?

134: What are the deployment features of .NET?

135: How can we create an array?

136: What is WCF?

137: What are the components of WCF?

138: What is the difference between array and arraylist?

139: Can we create custom controls?

140: List out the attributes that can be added for custom controls.

141: What is Bit Array?

142: How do we access crystal reports?

143: Explain the steps required to implement crystal reports.

144: Explain the difference between CTS and CLS.

145: What is the use of SCM?

146: What is a MaskedTextBox?

147: What are the components of Crystal Reports?

148: How to cast string to any data type?

149: List the fundamental objects of ADO.NET.

150: List the elements of .NET Framework.

151: Explain about shrinking session state.

152: What is Garbage Collection?

153: What is the role of Garbage Collector? Which method forces an immediate garbage collection of all generations?

154: How to display a number as percent?

155: How can we force to collect GC?

156: Explain how garbage collection manages reclamation of unused memory.

157: What is break mode?

158: What is WPF?

159: List the different documents supported in WPF.

160: What is XAML?

161: What is Windows Workflow Foundation?

162: What is LINQ?

163: What are different areas in which LINQ can be used?

164: Explain about Register Directive attributes.

165: Will the finally block get executed, if an exception occurs?

166: How can we throw an exception?

167: What is JSON.Net?

168: How do you split a string based on a character without using string.split function?

169: What is ELMAH?

170: Explain briefly how Passport authentication works.

171: What are the different ways in which WCF can be hosted?

172: What is ABC in WCF?

173: List the various contracts of WCF.

174: How can we achieve method overloading in WCF?

175: What are Destructors?

Web Application

176: Peter needs to create a web application for displaying the Welcome message to the user. What steps does he need to follow to achieve this task?

177: Explain in detail about the MVC architecture in C# web application.

178: What different controllers are present in the MVC hierarchy of an application?

179: Joe needs to pass the parameter from the controller to the view in the MVC architecture. What code should be added to transfer the values in the architecture?

180: What is the difference between ASP and ASP.NET?

181: What is IIS?

182: Explain about ASP.NET file.

183: What is an ASP.NET web form?

184: List out the ASP.NET page life cycle stages.

185: List out the various ASP.NET page life cycle events.

186: Explain about the PreInit event.

187: Explain about Page Request Stage.

188: What is a PostBack?

189: What is caching?

190:List out the different types of caching available in ASP.NET.

191: Explain about the stage Initialization.

192: What is a ViewState?

193: What is HttpHandler?

194: How can we improve the performance of ASP.NET page?

195: What is the use of GLOBAL.ASAX file?

196: What are user controls and custom controls?

197: What is a session and application object?

198: List the different types of directives available in .NET.

199: How can you prevent a browser from caching an ASPX page?

200: List out the validation controls available in ASP.NET.

201: What are the types of cookies available in ASP.NET?

202: List out the authentication techniques available in ASP.NET.

203: What is smart navigation?

204: What is State Management in ASP.NET?

205: List the different ASP.NET controls.

206: List the techniques available to store the state information in Client Side State Management.

207: What are the features of Grid View control?

208: List out the features of Data Grid.

209: What is a master page?

210: What is the difference between callbacks and postbacks?

211: How to copy contents of one dropdown list control to another dropdown control?

212: What is the use of AspCompat attribute?

213: How to load a control dynamically during runtime

214: Is it possible to get authentication mode during runtime?

215: List the event handlers that can be included in Global.asax file.

216: What is the difference between ResolveUrl and ResolveClientUrl?

217: Explain the AdRotator control.

218: List the elements of the AdRotator file.

219: Is it possible to pass multiple querystring parameters with hyperlink?

220: What is the easiest way to bring down any website?

221: How to print out all the variables in the Session?

222: What are the security threats for any website?

223: What are different ways with which hacking can be prevented?

224: Name few built in permission-sets in .NET.

225: What are the attributes available in <httpRuntime> node?

226: Give the code snippet of config file.

227: What is the use of @Page Directive?

228: Explain about the readystate property.

229: List the new features of ASP.NET 4 web forms.

Remoting and Webservices

230:Explain in brief about remoting in .net. List the different components of the remoting framework.

231: What criteria from communication options can be selected in a distributed application technology?

232: What is a web service? What are the different ways for web service development?

233: Create a web service to define the multiplication of three numbers in C#.

234: What is .NET Remoting?

235: What are two ways of creating remoting objects?

236: What is web service?

237: List out the components of web service.

238: What is SOAP?

239: What is WSDL?

240: What is DISCO?

241: What are the elements that should be contained in SOAP message?

242: List the elements that need to be described in WSDL for SOAP.

243: How can we make a method accessible through web service?

244: How do we deploy a web service?

245: How to consume a web service?

246: What are the data types supported in web services?

247: What are the common collection types used in C#? (1.2)

248: What the different phase/steps of acquiring a proxy object in Web service?

249: How to call a web service hosted in multiple servers dynamically during run time?

250: What do you mean by SOAP encoding?

251: Why should we Encrypt SOAP messages?

252: What is the difference between .NET Remoting and web services?

253: What is an application domain?

254: Explain about contexts.

255: What are remote objects?

256: List the main elements and attributes of system.runtime.remoting.

257: How can we stop a thread?

258: How to perform tracing/logging?

259: How to redirect tracing to a file?

260: Why strings are called immutable data types?

261: How to customize the serialization process?

262: What is WebClient?

263: How can we download files?

264: How to read contents of a file or URI using WebClient?

265: How can we upload files using WebClient?

266: What is Marshaling?

267: What is ObjRef object in Remoting?

268: How can we do windows authentication for web services?

269: Define declarative and imperative security.

270: What is DLL Hell?

271: What is a PE file?

272: How public key cryptography works?

273: Explain about refactoring of web.config.

274: What is Forms Authentication ticket?

275: What are the features of ASP.NET 4.0?

276: Define the term channel in .NET remoting.

277: What are remotable and non-remotable objects in Remoting?

278: List the different type of collections available in .NET.

279: What is Generic?

280: What are special collections?

281: Explain about CollectionsUtil.

282: Explain about ListCollection.

283: What are the different types of Generic collection?

284: How to use dictionary class?

HR Questions

1: Tell me about a time when you worked additional hours to finish a project.

2: Tell me about a time when your performance exceeded the duties and requirements of your job.

3: What is your driving attitude about work?

4: Do you take work home with you?

5: Describe a typical work day to me.

6: Tell me about a time when you went out of your way at your previous job.

7: Are you open to receiving feedback and criticisms on your job performance, and adjusting as necessary?

8: What inspires you?

9: How do you inspire others?

10: What has been your biggest success?

11: What motivates you?

12: What do you do when you lose motivation?

13: What do you like to do in your free time?

14: What sets you apart from other workers?

15: Why are you the best candidate for that position?

16: What does it take to be successful?

17: What would be the biggest challenge in this position for you?

18: Would you describe yourself as an introvert or an extrovert?

19: What are some positive character traits that you don't possess?

20: What is the greatest lesson you've ever learned?

21: Have you ever been in a situation where one of your strengths became a weakness in an alternate setting?

22: Who has been the most influential person in your life?

23: Do you consider yourself to be a "detailed" or "big picture" type of person?

24: What is your greatest fear?

50: If you could compare yourself to any animal, what would it be?

51: Who is your hero?

52: Who would play you in the movie about your life?

53: Name five people, alive or dead, that would be at your ideal dinner party.

54: What is customer service?

55: Tell me about a time when you went out of your way for a customer.

56: How do you gain confidence from customers?

57: Tell me about a time when a customer was upset or agitated – how did you handle the situation?

59: What would you do in a situation where you were needed by both a customer and your boss?

60: What is the most important aspect of customer service?

61: Is it best to create low or high expectations for a customer?

62: Why did you choose your college major?

63: Tell me about your college experience.

64: What is the most unique thing about yourself that you would bring to this position?

65: How did your last job stand up to your previous expectations of it?

66: How did you become interested in this field?

67: What was the greatest thing you learned while in school?

68: Tell me about a time when you had to learn a different skill set for a new position.

69: Tell me about a person who has been a great influence in your career.

70: What would this person tell me about you?

71: What is the most productive time of day for you?

72: What was the most responsibility you were given at your previous job?

73: Do you believe you were compensated fairly at your last job?

74: Tell me about a time when you received feedback on your work, and enacted it.

75: Tell me about a time when you received feedback on your work that you did not agree with, or thought was unfair. How did you handle it?

76: What was your favorite job, and why?

77: Tell me about an opportunity that your last position did not allow you to achieve.

78: Tell me about the worst boss you ever had.

Some of the following titles might also be handy:

1. .NET Interview Questions You'll Most Likely Be Asked
2. 200 Interview Questions You'll Most Likely Be Asked
3. Access VBA Programming Interview Questions You'll Most Likely Be Asked
4. Adobe ColdFusion Interview Questions You'll Most Likely Be Asked
5. Advanced Excel Interview Questions You'll Most Likely Be Asked
6. Advanced JAVA Interview Questions You'll Most Likely Be Asked
7. Advanced SAS Interview Questions You'll Most Likely Be Asked
8. AJAX Interview Questions You'll Most Likely Be Asked
9. Algorithms Interview Questions You'll Most Likely Be Asked
10. Android Development Interview Questions You'll Most Likely Be Asked
11. Ant & Maven Interview Questions You'll Most Likely Be Asked
12. Apache Web Server Interview Questions You'll Most Likely Be Asked
13. Artificial Intelligence Interview Questions You'll Most Likely Be Asked
14. ASP.NET Interview Questions You'll Most Likely Be Asked
15. Automated Software Testing Interview Questions You'll Most Likely Be Asked
16. Base SAS Interview Questions You'll Most Likely Be Asked
17. BEA WebLogic Server Interview Questions You'll Most Likely Be Asked
18. C & C++ Interview Questions You'll Most Likely Be Asked
19. C# Interview Questions You'll Most Likely Be Asked
20. C++ Internals Interview Questions You'll Most Likely Be Asked
21. CCNA Interview Questions You'll Most Likely Be Asked
22. Cloud Computing Interview Questions You'll Most Likely Be Asked
23. Computer Architecture Interview Questions You'll Most Likely Be Asked
24. Computer Networks Interview Questions You'll Most Likely Be Asked
25. Core JAVA Interview Questions You'll Most Likely Be Asked
26. Data Structures & Algorithms Interview Questions You'll Most Likely Be Asked
27. Data WareHousing Interview Questions You'll Most Likely Be Asked
28. EJB 3.0 Interview Questions You'll Most Likely Be Asked
29. Entity Framework Interview Questions You'll Most Likely Be Asked
30. Fedora & RHEL Interview Questions You'll Most Likely Be Asked
31. GNU Development Interview Questions You'll Most Likely Be Asked
32. Hibernate, Spring & Struts Interview Questions You'll Most Likely Be Asked
33. HTML, XHTML and CSS Interview Questions You'll Most Likely Be Asked
34. HTML5 Interview Questions You'll Most Likely Be Asked
35. IBM WebSphere Application Server Interview Questions You'll Most Likely Be Asked
36. iOS SDK Interview Questions You'll Most Likely Be Asked
37. Java / J2EE Design Patterns Interview Questions You'll Most Likely Be Asked
38. Java / J2EE Interview Questions You'll Most Likely Be Asked
39. Java Messaging Service Interview Questions You'll Most Likely Be Asked
40. JavaScript Interview Questions You'll Most Likely Be Asked
41. JavaServer Faces Interview Questions You'll Most Likely Be Asked
42. JDBC Interview Questions You'll Most Likely Be Asked
43. jQuery Interview Questions You'll Most Likely Be Asked
44. JSP-Servlet Interview Questions You'll Most Likely Be Asked
45. JUnit Interview Questions You'll Most Likely Be Asked
46. Linux Commands Interview Questions You'll Most Likely Be Asked
47. Linux Interview Questions You'll Most Likely Be Asked
48. Linux System Administrator Interview Questions You'll Most Likely Be Asked
49. Mac OS X Lion Interview Questions You'll Most Likely Be Asked
50. Mac OS X Snow Leopard Interview Questions You'll Most Likely Be Asked

51. Microsoft Access Interview Questions You'll Most Likely Be Asked
52. Microsoft Excel Interview Questions You'll Most Likely Be Asked
53. Microsoft Powerpoint Interview Questions You'll Most Likely Be Asked
54. Microsoft Word Interview Questions You'll Most Likely Be Asked
55. MySQL Interview Questions You'll Most Likely Be Asked
56. NetSuite Interview Questions You'll Most Likely Be Asked
57. Networking Interview Questions You'll Most Likely Be Asked
58. OOPS Interview Questions You'll Most Likely Be Asked
59. Operating Systems Interview Questions You'll Most Likely Be Asked
60. Oracle DBA Interview Questions You'll Most Likely Be Asked
61. Oracle E-Business Suite Interview Questions You'll Most Likely Be Asked
62. ORACLE PL/SQL Interview Questions You'll Most Likely Be Asked
63. Perl Programming Interview Questions You'll Most Likely Be Asked
64. PHP Interview Questions You'll Most Likely Be Asked
65. PMP Interview Questions You'll Most Likely Be Asked
66. Python Interview Questions You'll Most Likely Be Asked
67. RESTful JAVA Web Services Interview Questions You'll Most Likely Be Asked
68. Ruby Interview Questions You'll Most Likely Be Asked
69. Ruby on Rails Interview Questions You'll Most Likely Be Asked
70. SAP ABAP Interview Questions You'll Most Likely Be Asked
71. SAP HANA Interview Questions You'll Most Likely Be Asked
72. SAS Programming Guidelines Interview Questions You'll Most Likely Be Asked
73. Selenium Testing Tools Interview Questions You'll Most Likely Be Asked
74. Silverlight Interview Questions You'll Most Likely Be Asked
75. Software Repositories Interview Questions You'll Most Likely Be Asked
76. Software Testing Interview Questions You'll Most Likely Be Asked
77. SQL Server Interview Questions You'll Most Likely Be Asked
78. Tomcat Interview Questions You'll Most Likely Be Asked
79. UML Interview Questions You'll Most Likely Be Asked
80. Unix Interview Questions You'll Most Likely Be Asked
81. UNIX Shell Programming Interview Questions You'll Most Likely Be Asked
82. VB.NET Interview Questions You'll Most Likely Be Asked
83. Windows Server 2008 R2 Interview Questions You'll Most Likely Be Asked
84. XLXP, XSLT, XPATH, XFORMS & XQuery Interview Questions You'll Most Likely Be Asked
85. XML Interview Questions You'll Most Likely Be Asked

For complete list visit

www.vibrantpublishers.com

NOTES